WANDA E. BRUNSTETTER'S

Amish Friends

4 SEASONS

COOKBOOK

BARBOUR
PUBLISHING

© 2022 by Wanda E. Brunstetter

Print ISBN 978-1-63609-248-5

All scripture quotations are taken from the King James Version of the Bible.

First and Second Thumbnails: Doyle Yoder, dypinc.com

Published by Barbour Publishing, Inc., 1810 Barbour Drive, Uhrichsville, OH 44683, www.barbourbooks.com

Our mission is to inspire the world with the life-changing message of the Bible.

 Member of the Evangelical Christian Publishers Association

Printed in China.

Introduction

In my quest for good health, I learned many years ago that whenever possible, it's best to eat foods that are in season for the majority of my meals.

Seasonal food is produce purchased and eaten around the time that it is harvested. Seasonal food is fresher, has a better taste, and is more nutritious than food consumed out of season. Even though most people like to eat strawberries any time of the year, the best time to eat them is when they can be purchased from a local grower soon after harvest. Seasonal vegetables and fruits produced on local farms are fresher because they don't have to be shipped long distances. During the colder months, when food is not grown locally, I like to choose produce and other products that are shipped from areas as close to home as possible.

Eating foods that are in season is better for a person's health because the fruits and vegetables are nutritionally dense and taste better. Naturally ripened vegetables and fruits grown and picked in season are full of flavor and nutrients. Also, you can usually buy them at a lower price than when they are out of season.

My husband and I have a midsized garden, and we enjoy the fruits of our labors during the summer and fall months when the produce is ripe and ready to pick. If you are unable to grow a garden of your own, you might consider buying locally grown produce at farm stands or farmers' markets.

I hope you will enjoy the recipes in this cookbook that are served in Amish homes during each of the four seasons and on special holidays throughout the year.

A big thank-you goes to my editor, Rebecca Germany, and my granddaughter, Richelle, for their help in compiling the recipes and articles for this appetizing cookbook.

WANDA E. BRUNSTETTER

Thus hath the Lord
GOD shewed unto me:
and behold a basket
of summer fruit.

AMOS 8:1

CONTENTS

To every thing there is a season, and a time
to every purpose under the heaven: a time to be
born, and a time to die; a time to plant, and
a time to pluck up that which is planted.

ECCLESIASTES 3:1–2

The GENTLE FLOW of the SEASONS

Freshly cut grass! Fields of flowers and black soil overturned by a plow. Laundry flapping in the breeze. Spring is pushing your bare feet into the earth and feeling the soil squish through your toes and long straight rows of planted vegetables. Children running barefoot through the fields and grass, taking chances on the possibility of getting stung by bees feeding off the tiny flowers scattered throughout. Front porch chats with friends and family. Lovingly we share some of our first season's bounties—fresh peas, lettuce, onions, radishes, cucumbers, and peppers, to name a few. Those spring meals are light and fresh and mostly coming from the garden with some grilled meats added. Boiled new potatoes slathered with farm-fresh butter and topped with a creamy cucumber dressing made with mayo, sugar, vinegar, and salt. Some of the best light and healthy meals are from the early garden harvests!

Moving into summer, the harvests get bigger. Long, hard days of canning, soups, veggies, sauces, and relishes. Summer is roadside stands selling the excess, long warm days and swimming in the hole down by the creek, fishing, corn roasts, campfires, fellowship with family and friends while sharing our harvests. Tasty summer meals include corn on the cob, heirloom tomatoes sliced and made into sandwiches on large pieces of homemade bread slathered with mayonnaise. Burgers made outside over an open fire with freshly made relishes, refrigerator pickles, and pickled beets. Seasoned campfire potatoes and garden-fresh salad. Men taking a much-needed break as they go off fishing for a day and then gathering with neighbors for a meal of lightly breaded fish cooked in cast-iron pans.

Orchards are overflowing with apples and grapes. It means fall is here! Jars of applesauce and freshly pressed grape juice are quickly stored in the fruit cellar along with the summer's harvest. Neighbors gathering around copper kettles with bushels of apples, making apple butter. Fall means getting in one more campfire with s'mores, one more chilly swim, one more corn roast, and one more day in bare feet. Then it quickly turns into pumpkin pies and holidays with family and friends! Thanksgiving and Christmas dinners are turkey and ham, mashed potatoes and gravy, stuffing, creamed peas, and cranberry sauce with pumpkin and apple pies, date pudding, and gelatin salad, with tables set to capacity in the best chinaware. Family traveling in from other states by the van loads, each one bringing their own special side dish, dessert, or midday snack. A day of playing games and grab bags for Christmas gift exchanging. A day of catching up with the family news and exchanging letters from far-off friends and relatives.

As the last leaf falls to the ground and winter settles in, it's long days of sewing for the family, quilting, and knotting heavy comforters. Cleaning every inch of the house. Long cold days of butchering and preserving meats. Winter is skating and sledding parties with fires built to stay warm on those nights of outside play. It's evenings of games, popcorn, and tall glasses of grape juice. Gatherings around the table sharing laughter and friendship over canned soup and homemade bread. Meals turn into comfort foods to help keep us warmer on those cold days. Potato and chili soups, mashed potatoes, casseroles, canned meats, and vegetables taken from the root cellar. One by one the canned foods of summer disappear. Lots of freshly baked goods grace our tables. On a cold day outside, opening the door to the house as a wave of homemade cinnamon rolls or warm chocolate chip cookies hits the nostrils, then sitting down to enjoy with a cup of steaming coffee can't be beat.

Some of us live on "no winter maintenance" roads. Some live in populated areas. It makes no difference as we will continue to gather to share food and friendship. Whether you live in a city high-rise, a suburb, or a rural area, sharing friendship and laughter over a simple meal is recognized as love by all.

God bless each and every one of you as you continue to love and serve one another!

BETTY TROYER, Sarasota, FL

WHAT'S IN SEASON?

What does it mean to eat in season? Basically, it is just choosing to eat or preserve food, mainly fruits and vegetables, that are at their peak of freshness and ideally found locally so they aren't spending lots of time in transit. Peak season is also when you can usually expect the best price when buying in bulk due to abundance of the crop.

Here is a general list of the peak season for some of the common fruits and vegetables available to most of the United States.

Apples	fall
Asparagus	spring
Avocado	late summer through fall (Florida or California grown)
Beets	early summer through early winter
Blackberries	summer
Blueberries	summer
Broccoli	spring through fall
Brussels sprouts	fall
Cabbage	summer through early winter
Carrots	late spring through early winter
Cauliflower	summer through early winter
Celery	summer through early winter
Cherries	summer
Citrus (grapefruit, lemons, oranges)	late fall through early spring
Collard greens	fall
Corn	summer through fall
Cranberries	fall
Cucumbers	summer
Eggplant	summer
Fresh herbs	summer

Garlic	summer
Gooseberries	summer
Grapes	fall
Green beans	summer
Green onions	spring through summer
Kale	fall through early winter
Kiwi	winter (California grown)
Lettuce	spring through fall
Mangos	summer (Florida or California grown)
Melons	summer
Mushrooms	fall for common store-bought varieties
New potatoes	spring
Onions	summer through fall
Parsnips	fall
Peaches	summer
Pears	fall
Peas	spring
Pecans	summer
Peppers	summer through early fall
Pineapple	summer (Hawaii grown)
Potatoes	summer through fall
Pumpkin	fall
Radishes	spring through summer
Raspberries	summer
Rhubarb	late spring through early summer
Spinach	spring and fall
Strawberries	spring through summer
Summer squash	summer
Sweet potatoes	fall
Tomatoes	summer
Turnips	fall through winter
Wild greens (dandelion)	spring
Winter squash	fall

SPRING

Asparagus • Green Onions • Lettuce
New Potatoes • Peas • Radishes
Rhubarb • Spinach • Strawberries
Wild Greens (Dandelion)

SPRING RECIPES

"Dream as if you'll live forever.
Live as if you'll die tomorrow."

LEAH YODER, GLENVILLE, PA

RHUBARB DRINK

8 cups chopped rhubarb
8 cups water
2½ cups sugar
2 tablespoons
   strawberry gelatin

2 cups boiling water
2 cups pineapple juice
¼ cup lemon juice
6 cups ginger ale or
   lemon-lime soda pop

In a stockpot, bring rhubarb and water to a boil. Reduce heat. Simmer for 10 minutes. Drain, reserving liquid. In a large bowl, combine sugar, gelatin, and boiling water. Stir until dissolved. Add rhubarb liquid. Add pineapple juice and lemon juice. Refrigerate. Before serving, add soda pop.

You can also freeze or can the rhubarb base, but do not add pineapple juice, lemon juice, or pop until you are ready to use it. Then for every 1 quart juice, add 1 cup pineapple juice, ⅛ cup lemon juice, and 3 cups pop.

RACHEL SCHLABACH, Millersburg, OH

Rhubarb Tips

To get that sour or tart taste out of rhubarb, wash and cut the stalks. Place in a stainless-steel bowl and cover with boiling-hot water. Let set for an hour or more. Drain and use the rhubarb in your intended recipe. You can use the juice for a rhubarb drink by adding sugar and drink mix of your choice and taste. I always scald my rhubarb before I use it, and nobody complains of it being too sour or tart or bitter. This is also a way to use less sugar!

LENA TROYER, Redding, IA

If you have rocky soil and nothing much grows there, try planting rhubarb, especially if on the north side of a building. Cover plants thickly with horse manure after last frost for a good crop in spring. Harvest in months without r's (May, June, July, and August).

ESTHER L. MILLER, Fredericktown, OH

Strawberry Mizz Fizz

½ cup strawberries
¼ cup milk
¾ cup sugar
½ teaspoon vanilla

¼ cup strawberry or
  vanilla ice cream
¼ cup club soda

Blend strawberries, milk, sugar, vanilla, and ice cream in a blender. Then add soda in on-and-off pulsing motion until combined. Pour into chilled glass.

Mary Bontrager, Middlebury, IN

Strawberry Smoothie

3 bananas
1 pint strawberries
1 pint pineapple chunks
Handful blueberries

1 cup ice cubes
Splash coconut
  flavoring (optional)
Milk

In a blender, add bananas, strawberries, pineapple, blueberries, ice, and flavoring. Fill blender three-quarters full with milk. Blend until smooth. Add sugar only if you need to.

Anna Byler, Spartansburg, PA

Rhubarb Bread

1½ cups brown sugar
1 egg
⅔ cup vegetable oil
1 cup buttermilk
1 teaspoon vanilla
1 teaspoon baking soda

1 teaspoon salt
2½ cups flour
1½ cups diced rhubarb
½ cup sugar
1 tablespoon melted butter
¾ teaspoon cinnamon

Mix brown sugar, egg, oil, buttermilk, and vanilla. Add baking soda, salt, and flour. Fold in rhubarb. Do not overmix batter. Pour into 3 small greased bread pans. For topping, mix sugar, butter, and cinnamon. Sprinkle equally over each pan of batter. Bake at 325 degrees for 40 to 50 minutes.

"This is very moist and delicious bread."

FANNIE ANN HOSTETLER, Brookville, PA

STRAWBERRY SPINACH SALAD

3 to 4 cups torn spinach

1 bunch romaine
  lettuce, chopped

¾ quart sliced strawberries

¼ cup butter

1 package Ramen noodles

¼ cup crushed pecans

Place spinach and lettuce on a large plate. Top with strawberries. In a frying pan, melt butter. Crush noodles and add to butter along with pecans. Stir to toast until golden brown. Toss over salad just before serving and drizzle with dressing.

DRESSING:

¼ cup white vinegar

1 teaspoon salt

1 teaspoon mustard

1 teaspoon onion powder

1 cup oil

1 tablespoon poppy seeds

Mix vinegar, salt, mustard, and onion powder in a blender. While blending, drizzle in oil. When well combined, stop blender and stir in poppy seeds.

Optional: Add fresh blueberries along with the strawberries.

RANAE YODER, Kalona, IA

Dandelion Salad

3 slices bacon, cut small
2 tablespoons flour
2 teaspoons salt
1½ cups milk

4 cups washed and chopped
  dandelion leaves*
3 hard-boiled eggs, chopped

In a skillet, fry bacon until crispy. In a bowl, combine flour and salt. Mix in milk. Pour over bacon and cook until thickened. If too thick, add more milk. Cool slightly. In a bowl, mix dandelion and eggs. Pour dressing over dandelion and mix lightly.

* To remove bitter taste from dandelion, soak in salt water for 30 minutes. Drain well.

> *"Dandelion Salad is rich in protein, iron, calcium, phosphorus, and insulin."*

> MRS. LEVI MILLER, Junction City, OH

> *"I sometimes make a dandelion gravy with watercress, spinach, or kale in place of dandelion."*

> ANNA M. BYLER, Commodore, PA

Dandelion Flowers

Big dandelion flowers
2 beaten eggs
⅓ cup milk

Seasoned flour
Bacon grease, shortening,
  oil, or butter

Pick nice big dandelion flowers in whatever amount you need. Check for bugs and shake a bit. Mix eggs and milk. Dip flowers in mixture. Let drain a bit then dip in seasoned flour. Fry in bacon grease (best for flavor) flower-side down first, then turn over. Drain on paper towels.

> ESTHER L. MILLER, Fredericktown, OH

Early Spring Salad

4 cups young red beet leaves
1 cup peas
¼ cup sliced radishes
¼ cup sliced young
    cucumbers

1 cup shredded cheese
¾ cup bacon bits
Sprinkle lemon
    pepper (optional)

Dice beet leaves into a bowl. Sprinkle in peas. Arrange radishes and cucumbers on top. Sprinkle with cheese and bacon bits. Sprinkle with lemon pepper. Dab spoonfuls of dressing on top.

DRESSING:

6 ounces sour cream
1 tablespoon sugar

1 cup ranch dressing
Salt and pepper to taste

Mix sour cream, sugar, and ranch dressing. Season with salt and pepper to taste.

KATIE SCHMIDT, Carlisle, KY

Springtime Swiss Cashew Salad

1 medium head romaine
    lettuce, chopped
1 cup salted cashews

4 ounces grated swiss cheese
8 to 10 strawberries, sliced
1 small red onion, sliced

Combine all in a large bowl. Add dressing just before serving.

DRESSING:

⅓ cup vinegar
¾ cup sugar
2 teaspoons mustard
⅛ teaspoon salt

1 teaspoon chopped
    onion or onion flakes
1 cup vegetable oil
1 teaspoon poppy seeds

Mix all well.

JOANN MILLER, Fredericktown, OH

Asparagus Tips

Young, slender, firm stalks with closed compact tips are the best. All the green part should be tender and edible after cooking. The white part should be cut away before cooking but may be saved for flavoring soups and stews. It is a fairly perishable vegetable. Once cut, it ages fast. Wilted asparagus has opened tips, which may be discolored, and tough, leathery stalks.

KATHRYN DETWEILER, West Farmington, OH

ASPARAGUS WITH DILL BUTTER

2½ pounds asparagus
Boiling water
1½ teaspoons salt, divided
½ cup melted butter, divided
2 egg yolks

¼ cup water
1½ tablespoons lemon juice
1 tablespoon fresh
  snipped dill

Break or cut off tough ends of asparagus; wash well. Bunch stalks together in 4 to 6 groups and tie with string. Place upright in deep saucepan. Cover with 2 inches of boiling water and add 1½ teaspoons of salt. Cook 15 minutes. Drain well. Arrange on heated serving dish. Pour ¼ cup of butter over asparagus. Combine remaining ¼ cup butter with remaining ¼ teaspoon salt, egg yolks, ¼ cup water, lemon juice, and dill. Heat and serve over asparagus. Yields 4 to 6 servings.

"Tender shoots of asparagus bring a little taste of spring to any table. This is a single quick dish to serve at a dinner party."

KATHRYN DETWEILER, West Farmington, OH

Asparagus and Bacon

2 cups cut asparagus
2 cups chopped bacon

Brown together in frying pan until asparagus is tender.

Crystal Ropp, Kalona, IA

Buttered Asparagus

2 cups broken asparagus   1 teaspoon salt
1 tablespoon butter   ½ teaspoon pepper

Cook asparagus in butter over low heat until asparagus is soft. Add salt and pepper. Serve.

Rosa C. Schmidt, Carlisle, KY

CRISPY ASPARAGUS STICKS

Asparagus spears
Salt

Olive oil

Wash and dry asparagus and lay flat on a baking sheet. Sprinkle with salt to taste. Sprinkle a little oil to lightly coat the asparagus. Broil until nice and crispy. May require some turning.

LEAH YODER, Glenville, PA

SUGARED ASPARAGUS

3 tablespoons butter
  or margarine
2 tablespoons brown sugar

2 pounds fresh asparagus,
  cut into 2-inch pieces
  (about 4 cups)
1 cup chicken broth

In a skillet over medium-high heat, melt butter and sugar until sugar is dissolved. Add asparagus and sauté for 2 minutes. Stir in chicken broth. Bring to a boil. Reduce heat. Cover and simmer for 8 to 10 minutes or until asparagus is crisp and tender. Remove asparagus to a serving dish and cover to keep warm. Continue to cook liquids in skillet uncovered until reduced by half. Pour over asparagus and serve. Yield: 4 to 6 servings.

MRS. REUBEN (MARTHA) BYLER, Atlantic, PA

BAKED ASPARAGUS

2 (16 ounce) cans, drained,
  or fresh cooked-to-
  tender asparagus
4 hard-boiled eggs, chopped
2 cups shredded cheese

1 can cream of
  mushroom soup
1 cup milk
¼ cup butter
2 cups breadcrumbs

In a casserole, layer 1 can asparagus, 2 eggs, and 1 cup cheese. Repeat layers. In a bowl, combine soup and milk. Pour over contents of casserole. In another bowl, mix butter with breadcrumbs. Sprinkle over casserole. Bake at 350 degrees for 30 minutes.

NATHAN AND ANNA FISHER, Salisbury, PA

HERBED NEW POTATOES

12 small new potatoes
4 teaspoons butter
4 teaspoons minced
    fresh parsley or 1⅓
    teaspoons dried

4 teaspoons minced
    fresh chives or 1⅓
    teaspoons dried
Fresh parsley sprigs
    (optional for garnish)

Peel a ½-inch strip around center of each potato and immediately place potatoes in a medium saucepan of cold water. Add enough additional water to cover potatoes by 2 inches. Bring to a boil over medium-high heat. Boil about 20 minutes until potatoes are easily pierced by a fork but still firm. Do not overcook. Drain. Cover to keep warm. In a small pan, melt butter and stir in parsley and chives. Pour mixture over potatoes and toss to coat. Spoon potatoes into a serving bowl and garnish with sprigs of parsley, if desired. Serve immediately. Serves 4.

For variety, sprinkle with chopped, cooked bacon and/or finely minced green onions.

MARY ANN YUTZY, Bloomfield, IA

SAUTÉED RADISHES

¼ cup butter
1 pound radishes, sliced
Salt to taste

In a frying pan, heat butter. Add radishes. Cook, stirring often, until nicely browned. Salt to taste.

"Anita, age 6, came up with this recipe on her own to the delight of her family."

ANITA LORRAINE PETERSHEIM, Fredericktown, OH

Spring Garden Soup

6 tablespoons butter
3 green onions, thinly sliced
6 tablespoons flour
3 cups milk
2 cups chicken broth

½ cup thinly sliced carrots
1½ cups fresh peas
1 cup chopped fresh spinach
Salt and pepper to taste

In a saucepan, melt butter and sauté onion until tender but not brown. Stir in flour and cook until smooth, stirring constantly. Remove from heat. Gradually stir in milk and broth. Bring to a boil over medium heat, stirring constantly for 1 minute. Add carrots, peas, and spinach. Simmer uncovered, stirring occasionally, until vegetables are tender. Add salt and pepper to taste.

Rosie E. Schwartz, Berne, IN

FRESH ASPARAGUS SOUP

1 pound fresh asparagus,
  chopped
¼ cup chopped onion
2 cups chicken broth, divided
2 tablespoons butter
  or margarine
2 tablespoons flour

½ teaspoon salt
Dash pepper
1 cup milk
½ cup sour cream or
  plain yogurt
1 teaspoon fresh lemon juice
Chopped chives

Cook asparagus and onion in 1 cup chicken broth in a covered saucepan. When asparagus is just tender, press through a food mill or blend until smooth. (I don't always do this.) In another saucepan, melt butter. Stir in flour, salt, and pepper. Add remaining 1 cup chicken broth. Cook over medium heat, stirring constantly, until mixture reaches boiling point. Add asparagus puree and milk. In a bowl, stir a little hot mixture into sour cream to warm it, then add to soup along with lemon juice. Heat to serving temperature, stirring frequently. Sprinkle with some chives to serve.

LENA TROYER, Redding, IA

Asparagus Hamburger Potato Soup

3 to 4 tablespoons butter
2 cups asparagus cut
   into pea-sized pieces
3 to 4 tablespoons flour
Salt and pepper to taste

2 medium potatoes, cut
   into ½-inch cubes
½ teaspoon salt
1 pound hamburger,
   fried and drained
2 quarts milk

In a frying pan, melt butter. Add asparagus and cook until tender. Sprinkle flour over asparagus and salt and pepper to taste. Fry a little then set aside. In a 4-quart saucepan, cover potatoes with water. Add ½ teaspoon salt. Bring to a boil until potatoes are tender, not mushy. Then add hamburger and asparagus. Add milk and salt and pepper to taste. Bring to a boil and serve with crackers.

MARY BONTRAGER, Middlebury, IN

Asparagus Cheese Strata

2 pounds fresh
   asparagus, cut fine
3 tablespoons butter, melted
1 pound sliced bread
2 cups finely diced
   cooked ham

¾ cup shredded cheese
4 eggs
½ teaspoon salt
3 cups milk
1 small onion

In a saucepan, cook asparagus in a little water until tender. In a 9x13 pan, coat bottom and sides with butter. Lay slices of bread on bottom of pan. Cover with asparagus, ham, and half of the cheese. Top with sliced bread. In a bowl, beat eggs, salt, and milk. Pour over bread. Sprinkle with remaining half of cheese. Layer sliced onion on top. Bake at 375 degrees for 50 minutes.

DORCAS MARIE YODER, Meyersdale, PA

ASPARAGUS AND PEA CASSEROLE

1½ pounds fresh asparagus, trimmed and broken

2 cups fresh peas or 1 (10 ounce) package frozen peas

¾ cup sliced fresh mushrooms, or 1 small can sliced mushrooms, drained

1 (2 ounce) jar diced pimiento, drained

3 tablespoons butter

3 tablespoons flour

¾ cup milk

1 (5 ounce) jar sharp processed cheese

¼ teaspoon salt

⅛ teaspoon pepper

½ cup fine dry breadcrumbs

3 tablespoons melted butter

Cook asparagus in water until tender. Drain, reserving ¾ cup asparagus liquid. Set liquid aside. Place asparagus in a lightly greased 12x8x2-inch casserole dish. Cook peas according to directions on package; drain well. Place peas over asparagus. Layer mushrooms and pimiento over peas. Set aside.

Melt 3 tablespoons butter in a saucepan over low heat. Add flour, stirring until smooth. Cook 1 minute. Combine ¾ cup asparagus liquid with milk. Gradually add to cooked flour. Cook over medium heat, stirring constantly until mixture is bubbly and thick. Stir in cheese, salt, and pepper. Pour over vegetables in casserole. Combine breadcrumbs and melted butter. Sprinkle over sauce. Cover and refrigerate 8 hours or overnight. Remove and let stand 30 minutes at room temperature. Bake at 350 degrees, uncovered, for 40 minutes or until heated through.

LENA TROYER, Redding, IA

FRIED FROG LEGS

Fresh hind legs of frogs
Lemon juice
Salt and pepper to taste
Flour

Egg, beaten
Cracker crumbs
Fat
Tartar sauce

Skin legs by turning skin inside out and pulling down to smallest end. Wipe with a cold damp cloth. Soak legs in lemon juice, salt, and pepper 1 hour before preparing. Shake off excess liquid. Roll in flour. Dip into beaten egg thinned with a little water. Roll in cracker crumbs. (You could also substitute fritter batter for flour, egg, and cracker crumbs.) Fry in deep hot fat until golden brown, about 3 minutes. Serve with tartar sauce.

AMANDA HERSHBERGER, Fredericksburg, OH

Rhubarb Cake with Frosting

2 cups diced rhubarb
2 cups sugar, divided
½ cup shortening
1 egg
1 cup sour cream
2 cups flour

Dash salt
1 teaspoon baking soda
1 teaspoon cinnamon
1 teaspoon vanilla
Powdered sugar

In a bowl, mix rhubarb with ½ cup sugar. In another bowl, cream remaining 1½ cups sugar with shortening. Add egg and sour cream. Add flour, salt, baking soda, cinnamon, and vanilla. Fold in rhubarb. Pour into a greased 9x13-inch pan. Bake at 350 degrees for 30 minutes until done. Sprinkle top with powdered sugar. Yummy as is, or you can use this frosting on cooled cake.

Frosting:

½ cup butter, softened
8 ounces cream cheese

4 cups powdered sugar
1 teaspoon vanilla

In a bowl, cream butter and cream cheese. Beat in powdered sugar and vanilla until smooth. Spread over cake.

BETHANY MARTIN, Homer City, PA

Rhubarb Coffee Cake with Sauce

Batter:

¾ cup butter

1½ cups sugar

1 large or 2 small eggs

1⅛ cups milk

3 cups flour

4½ teaspoons baking powder

¾ teaspoon salt

3 cups chopped rhubarb

½ cup brown sugar

½ teaspoon cinnamon

¼ teaspoon nutmeg

In a bowl, cream together butter and sugar. Add egg, milk, flour, baking powder, and salt. Fold in rhubarb. Spread in 9x13-inch greased pan. In a bowl, mix brown sugar, cinnamon, and nutmeg. Sprinkle over batter. Bake at 350 degrees for 30 to 40 minutes until a toothpick comes out clean.

Sauce:

2 eggs, beaten

2 cups sugar

1 cup heavy cream

¼ cup butter

2 teaspoons vanilla

In a heavy saucepan, combine eggs, sugar, and cream. Cook over low heat until boiling, stirring constantly. Boil 1 minute. Remove from heat; add butter and vanilla. Drizzle hot sauce over warm cake to serve.

Esther Miller, Rossiter, PA

Rhubarb Crunch

1 cup flour

¾ cup oats

1 cup brown sugar

½ cup melted butter

1 teaspoon cinnamon

4 cups diced rhubarb

1 cup sugar

1 cup water

2 tablespoons cornstarch

1 teaspoon vanilla

Mix flour, oatmeal, brown sugar, butter, and cinnamon until crumbly. Press half of crumbs into a 9-inch pan. Cover with rhubarb. In a saucepan, cook together sugar, water, cornstarch, and vanilla until clear. Pour over rhubarb. Top with remaining half of crumbs. Bake at 350 degrees for 45 minutes or until rhubarb is tender.

Kari Danette Petersheim, Fredericktown, OH

RHUBARB CHEESECAKE BARS

CRUST:

2 cups flour

¾ cup powdered sugar

1 cup butter

In a bowl, mix flour and sugar. Cut in butter until crumbly. Press into 9x13-inch pan. Bake at 350 degrees for 15 minutes. Prepare filling while crust bakes.

FILLING:

4 eggs

2 cups sugar

½ cup flour

½ teaspoon salt

4 cups diced rhubarb

In a bowl, beat eggs with sugar. Mix in flour and salt. Stir in rhubarb. Pour over hot crust and bake at 350 degrees for 45 minutes. Cool completely before adding topping.

TOPPING:

1 (8 ounce) package
   cream cheese

½ cup sugar

½ teaspoon vanilla

1 (8 ounce) tub
   whipped topping

In a small bowl, beat cream cheese, sugar, and vanilla. Add whipped topping and beat until smooth. Spread over cooled rhubarb. Chill. Cut into bars to serve.

SADIE GLICK, Howard, PA

RHUBARB TORTE

CRUST:

¾ cup butter at room temperature

2 cups flour

¼ cup sugar

Mix all until crumbly. Pat in 9x13-inch pan. Bake at 350 degrees for 12 minutes.

CUSTARD:

5 cups finely cut rhubarb

6 egg yolks

2 cups sugar

6 tablespoons flour

1 cup cream

¼ cup milk

1 heaping tablespoon sour cream

In a saucepan, partially cook rhubarb with a little water until soft; drain. Mix in egg yolks, sugar, flour, cream, milk, and sour cream; pour over crust. Bake at 350 degrees for 40 minutes until custard is set.

TOPPING:

6 egg whites

½ cup sugar

¼ teaspoon salt

1 teaspoon vanilla

¼ teaspoon cream of tartar

In a bowl, beat egg whites until stiff. Gradually add sugar, salt, vanilla, and cream of tartar. Spread over custard and continue baking for 10 to 15 minutes until egg whites are nice and brown.

"This is so delicious. I get hungry for it before my rhubarb is ready to pick. So if I have extra in the summer, I freeze some. Put 5 cups chopped rhubarb in a bag, freeze, and then it will be ready to use."

RACHEL SCHLABACH, Millersburg, OH

French Rhubarb Pie

1 cup sugar
2 tablespoons flour
Pinch salt
1 egg, beaten
2 cups diced rhubarb
½ teaspoon vanilla

¼ cup sour cream
1 (9 inch) unbaked pie shell
¾ cup flour
¼ cup brown sugar
⅓ cup butter

In a bowl, mix sugar, 2 tablespoons flour, and salt. Add egg, rhubarb, vanilla, and sour cream. Blend well. Pour into pie shell. In a bowl, mix ¾ cup flour, brown sugar, and butter until crumbly. Sprinkle crumbs over filling. Bake at 375 degrees for 40 minutes.

JOANNA D. MILLER, Loudonville, OH

Strawberry Rhubarb Delight

1 quart rhubarb
3 cups water
½ cup tapioca
1 cup sugar
Pinch baking soda

1 (3 ounce) box
   strawberry gelatin
1 quart sliced strawberries
1 (8 ounce) container
   whipped topping

In a 4-quart saucepan, cook rhubarb, water, tapioca, sugar, and baking soda until tapioca is clear. Then add gelatin, stirring until dissolved. Add strawberries. Chill thoroughly. Fold in whipped topping.

MARY BONTRAGER, Middlebury, IN

BERRIES ON A CLOUD

MERINGUE CRUST:

6 egg whites

½ teaspoon cream of tartar

1½ cups sugar

1 teaspoon vanilla

Beat egg whites and cream of tartar until peaks form. Add sugar and vanilla and beat until it is not grainy. Cut out a paper bag to the size of your large cookie sheet. Put paper on the sheet and evenly spread egg white mixture on paper. Bake at 200 degrees for 1½ hours. Do not open oven while baking. When bake time ends, turn off heat and keep oven closed 1 hour.

FILLING:

1 (8 ounce) package cream cheese

¼ cup sugar

1 (8 ounce) container whipped topping

Beat together cream cheese and sugar until smooth. Mix in whipped topping. Spread over cooled crust.

TOPPING:

2 cups strawberry glaze

4 cups sliced fresh strawberries

Spread glaze over cream cheese mixture. Top with strawberries.

MRS. MOSE K. SCHWARTZ, Geneva, IN

FRESH STRAWBERRY PIE

CRUST:

¾ cup flour
½ cup quick oats
½ cup chopped pecans

2 tablespoons sugar
⅛ teaspoon salt
½ cup melted butter

In a bowl, combine flour, oats, pecans, sugar, and salt. Stir in butter until blended. Press onto the bottom and up the sides of 9-inch pie pan. Bake at 400 degrees for 12 to 15 minutes. Cool.

FILLING:

¾ cup sugar
2 tablespoons cornstarch
1 cup water
2 tablespoons light
  corn syrup

2 tablespoons strawberry
  gelatin powder
1 quart fresh
  strawberries, sliced

Meanwhile, combine sugar and cornstarch in a saucepan, then gradually beat in water and corn syrup. Bring to boil over medium heat. Cook and stir for 2 minutes. Remove from heat and stir in gelatin until dissolved. Cool. Arrange berries over crust. Pour gelatin mixture over berries. Refrigerate 2 hours or until set. Serve with whipped cream.

WHIPPED CREAM:

1 cup whipping cream
2 tablespoons sugar

¼ teaspoon almond flavoring

In a mixing bowl, beat cream with sugar and almond flavoring until stiff peaks form.

"Nothing sweetens a warm spring day like a piece of this delicious strawberry pie. The best in the country!"

KATHRYN DETWEILER, West Farmington, OH

FRESH STRAWBERRY PIZZA

CRUST:

1¼ cups flour
½ cup margarine or butter
¾ cup chopped pecans
3 tablespoons sugar

In a bowl, mix flour, butter, pecans, and sugar. Press into a 9x13-inch pan. Bake at 350 degrees for 20 minutes. Cool.

FILLING:

1 cup margarine or butter, melted
1 (8 ounce) package cream cheese
2 cups powdered sugar
1 teaspoon vanilla

In a mixing bowl, cream margarine, cream cheese, sugar, and vanilla until light and fluffy. Spread over cooled crust. Cover and chill for 2 to 3 hours.

TOPPING:

1 cup sugar
3 tablespoons cornstarch
2 teaspoons lemon juice
1 cup water
3 tablespoons strawberry gelatin
2 quarts fresh strawberries, sliced
1 (8 ounce) container whipped topping

In a saucepan, combine sugar, cornstarch, lemon juice, water, and gelatin. Boil until thick. Stir in strawberries. Spread over filling. Chill. Top with whipped topping.

DORCAS MARIE YODER, Meyersdale, PA

Strawberry Shortcake

¾ cup sugar
¼ cup vegetable oil
  or shortening
1 egg
½ cup milk
1½ cups flour

2 teaspoons baking powder
½ teaspoon salt
½ cup brown sugar
2 tablespoons flour
2 tablespoons butter

In a bowl, mix sugar and oil. Stir in egg and milk. Add 1½ cups flour, baking powder, and salt. Pour into a greased 8x8-inch pan. In a bowl, mix together brown sugar, 2 tablespoons flour, and butter to form crumbs. Place on top of batter. Bake at 325 degrees for 30 minutes. Delicious served with strawberries when they are fresh and in season.

Rebecca Stutzman, Dalton, OH

Strawberry Yum Yum

2 cups flour
½ cup brown sugar
¾ cup butter
4 egg whites

1½ cups sugar
2 cups heavy cream
4 cups chopped fresh
  strawberries

In a bowl, cream flour, brown sugar, and butter. Press lightly into 9x13-inch pan. Bake at 350 degrees for 20 minutes. Let cool. In a bowl, beat egg whites to slightly stiff then add sugar and beat to stiff peaks. In another bowl, beat cream until thickened and peaked. Fold cream into egg whites. Fold in strawberries. Pour on top of cooled crust and freeze.

"A very refreshing spring dessert."

Crystal Ropp, Kalona, IA

RHUBARB PIE FILLING (TO CAN)

14 cups chopped rhubarb
1 gallon plus 3 quarts water
1 teaspoon salt
12 cups sugar
2 tablespoons lemon juice

4 cups Perma Flo
5 cups water
1 large can crushed
pineapple
1½ cups strawberry gelatin

In a stockpot, bring rhubarb, water, salt, sugar, and lemon juice to boil. Add Perma Flo mixed with 5 cups water. Bring all to a boil to thicken, then add pineapple and gelatin. Fill jars and process in hot water bath for 15 minutes. Makes 14 quarts.

Note: This is also good on ice cream as a topping.

MARY AND KATIE YODER, Goshen, IN

Strawberry Jam

12 cups crushed strawberries
22 cups sugar

2 cups fruit pectin
1 quart water

In a large bowl, mix strawberries and sugar, stirring until sugar dissolves. In a large pot, mix fruit pectin and water. Bring to a boil that cannot be stirred down, then let boil for 1 minute. Add strawberry mixture and stir over heat for 3 minutes. Put into jars and let stand for 24 hours. Cold-pack jars for 5 minutes to seal. Makes 16 pints.

Lydia Hershberger, Dalton, OH

Dandelion Jelly

1 quart dandelion blossoms,
  no stems attached
1 quart water
1¼ packages Sure-Jell or
  pectin (approx. ¼ cup total)

1 teaspoon lemon or
  orange extract
4½ cups sugar

Wash blossoms, then boil in water for 3 minutes. Drain off 3 cups cooking liquid into a saucepan. Discard blossoms. To liquid, add Sure-Jell, lemon extract, and sugar. Boil for 5 minutes. Pour into jelly jars and seal in hot water bath.

"A fun jelly to make in spring before anything in the garden is ready."

Joann Miller, Fredericktown, OH

Susan C. Schwartz, Berne, IN

Rhubarb Jelly

5 cups finely chopped
  rhubarb
4 cups sugar

1 large package gelatin
  (flavor your choice)

Combine rhubarb and sugar and let set overnight. In the morning, bring mixture to a boil for 5 minutes. Remove from heat and add gelatin, stirring until dissolved. Portion into containers. Refrigerate or freeze.

Mrs. Mose K. Schwartz, Geneva, IN

Strawberry-Rhubarb Jelly

5 cups finely chopped
  rhubarb
5 cups sugar

2 cups crushed pineapple
1 large package
  strawberry gelatin

Combine rhubarb, sugar, and pineapple and let set overnight. In the morning, bring mixture to a boil and cook about 20 minutes until tender. Remove from heat and add gelatin, stirring until dissolved. Portion into containers. Refrigerate or freeze.

Mrs. Lizzie Schwartz, Geneva, IN

Spring Cleaning Tips

House Cleaner

2 cups water
15 drops lemon or
    lavender essential oil

15 drops rosemary
    essential oil
15 drops tea tree oil

In a spray bottle, mix water with oils. Shake bottle before each use.

Ruthie Miller, Loudonville, OH

Shower Cleaner

⅓ cup Dawn
    dishwashing soap

12 ounces white vinegar
Water

Combine soap and vinegar in quart-sized spray bottle. Fill bottle with water. Use to clean showers and sinks. Works great to cut soap scum.

Ruth Hochstetler, Dundee, OH

Citrus Dusting Spray

2 teaspoons olive oil
1 teaspoon lemon
    or orange oil

¼ cup vinegar
1 cup water

Combine all in a spray bottle. Use to spray on a piece of cheesecloth and then wipe wooden furniture. A little goes a long way. Mix well before each use.

Ada J. Mast, Kalona, IA

Mildew Remover

2 quarts water
½ cup vinegar

½ cup bleach

Combine ingredients. Soak mildew spots several hours or overnight. Rinse and dry.

Anna Zook, Dalton, OH

WINDOWS

To clean windows and mirrors with streaks, wipe the cleaner off with newspaper instead of paper towels.

CRYSTAL ROPP, Kalona, IA

MARK REMOVER

Use lemon oil to take permanent marker, crayon, or scuff marks off floors, walls, etc.

MARY ELLEN MILLER, Apple Creek, OH

CLEANING WITH BRUSHES

Paintbrushes are handy for dusting louvered doors, lamp shades, and baseboards. Toothbrushes are great for cleaning hard-to-get places such as tile grout, faucets, knobs, shirt cuffs and collars, graters, colanders, etc.

RACHEL KUEFER, Kincardine, Ontario

All the Seasons Have Special Blessings!

SPRING AND SUMMER

Soon after winter's snow melts, everything wakes up from its dormant stage. One of the things you see first (in February in northern Indiana) is the tapping of maple trees. Yes, the maple syrup, which weighs 11 pounds per gallon, requires lots of hard work. If one has never cooked maple syrup, you'd be interested to know that in the average year, it takes 40 gallons of sap (as it comes out of the tree) to make 1 gallon of maple syrup. Once all the gathering and cooking is done, you may soon decide paying $40-$50 dollars per gallon isn't all that expensive. And nothing beats pure maple syrup on pancakes or waffles.

Why do they tap maple trees only in the spring? Because as the sap moves up and out to the tree branches, that's when you can get the sap. "Nature's wonders" store the sap in the roots and the lower tree trunk to keep it alive through the cold weather. Another fact about "Nature's wonders" is the trees will only give what they can spare. Usually the season is 2 to 3 weeks long. After that, the sap will turn cloudy and will no longer be sweet. This is all in God's design.

Also in early spring, the crocuses, hyacinths, and daffodils show their brilliant colors. Birds take their long journeys from south to north.

Good Friday and Easter are very important holidays for all mankind. On Good Friday, the day of Jesus' crucifixion, Jesus shed enough blood for all of our sins. Then Easter morning, the third day, Jesus arose from the grave–alive! Easter is a special family time!

Forty days after Easter, Jesus ascended into heaven. He has not yet come back to get His followers.

The next two special days are Mother's Day in May and Father's Day in June. These two days are for us to stop and thank our parents for our care and heritage. It's a great gift to us if we choose to celebrate.

With spring and summer come lots of outside work, including planting gardens and flowers, mowing lawns, and hoeing weeds. There's also canning and freezing fruits and veggies to enjoy during the winter.

Summertime fun can be camping, hiking, and ball games with family and friends. Thanks to God for all the precious memories!

K.Y., Goshen, IN

SUMMER

Beets · Blackberries · Blueberries · Broccoli
Cauliflower · Celery · Cherries · Corn · Cucumbers
Eggplant · Fresh Herbs · Gooseberries · Green Beans
Mango · Melon · Peaches · Pineapple
Raspberries · Summer Squash · Tomatoes

SUMMER RECIPES

"Happiness is like jam; you can't spread it
without getting some on yourself."
RHODA MILLER, DECATUR, IN

Fuzzy Naval Smoothie

¾ cup chopped fresh
    peaches or nectarines

1 cup ice cubes

Place peaches and ice in a blender and blend until desired consistency. Enjoy immediately.

SUSANNA MAST, Kalona, IA

Watermelon Refresher

3 to 4 cups cubed,
    chilled watermelon

1 cup water
Squeeze fresh lime juice

Put all ingredients in blender and blend until smooth.

SADIE GLICK, Howard, PA

Blueberry Smoothie

1 cup fresh blueberries
1 banana
¼ cup yogurt
¼ cup milk

½ cup pineapple or
    orange juice
Pinch cinnamon

In a blender, blend all together until smooth. Serve immediately. Makes 1 serving.

BARBIE STOLTZFOOS, Oxford, PA

Raspberry Lemonade

1½ cups raspberries
1 cup lemon juice

1 cup water
Sweetener to taste

In blender, blend raspberries, lemon juice, and water. Strain. Put juice in a 2-quart pitcher and fill with water and ice.

Optional: Use ⅓ to ½ cup sugar-free raspberry syrup instead of raspberries.

NORMA YUTZY, Drakesville, IA

Summer Iced Tea

12 quarts water
5 pounds sugar
5 cups lemon juice

75 mint tea leaves
15 regular tea bags

In a large stockpot, simmer all together for 30 minutes. Cool. Pour into quart canning jars and seal in a water bath. To use: dilute 1 quart of tea with 1 quart of water and ice.

ANNA BYLER, Spartansburg, PA
MRS. REBECCA BYLER, Spartansburg, PA

Mango-Pineapple Smoothie

1 whole ripe mango,
   peeled and pitted
½ can pineapple chunks
Handful spinach

½ cup ice
½ teaspoon vanilla
Stevia, if desired

Put all ingredients in blender and blend on high for 1 minute. Enjoy!

RANAE YODER, Kalona, IA

Simple Summertime Milkshake

Ice cube tray filled with
   milk and frozen
2 cups milk

1 to 1½ cups fresh fruit
⅓ to ½ cup sugar

In a blender, add frozen milk cubes, milk, fruit, and sugar. Blend on high speed until well mixed. Enjoy immediately for a delicious summertime drink. Yields 6 cups. This is also good without the frozen milk and can be beaten with eggbeater to blend.

RUTH M. YODER, Berlin, PA

FRUIT DIP

1 (8 ounce) package cream
  cheese, softened
½ cup powdered sugar
1 (8 ounce) container
  whipped topping

1 (16 ounce) carton
  strawberry yogurt (or any
  flavor you desire)

In a bowl, blend cream cheese and sugar. Beat in whipped topping and yogurt until smooth. Serve with fresh fruits.

MARILYN LAMBRIGHT, Goshen, IN

FRESH GARDEN SALSA

4 cups diced tomatoes,
  drained well in colander
½ cup very finely diced onions
1 large green bell
  pepper, diced
2 cups diced cucumber
½ cup chopped fresh parsley

¼ cup chopped fresh cilantro
1 tablespoon vinegar
1 tablespoon lemon juice
½ teaspoon cumin
Dash pepper

Mix all together and refrigerate 4 hours before serving. Very refreshing and goes well served with corn chips or tacos.

Variation: Add 2 cups fresh-cut corn and 1 can black beans, drained and rinsed.

KATHRYN TROYER, Rutherford, TN

BLT BITES

16 to 20 cherry tomatoes
1 pound bacon, cooked
  and crumbled
½ cup mayonnaise or
  salad dressing

⅓ cup chopped green onion
3 tablespoons grated cheddar
  or Parmesan cheese
2 tablespoons snipped
  fresh parsley

Cut thin slice off each tomato top. Scoop out and discard pulp. Invert tomatoes on paper towel to drain. In a small bowl, combine bacon, mayonnaise, green onion, cheese, and parsley. Mix well. Spoon mixture into tomatoes. Refrigerate several hours before serving. Rather time-consuming but delicious.

NORMA YUTZY, Drakesville, IA

Blueberry Mini Muffins

1 cup butter or
   margarine, softened
2 cups sugar
5 eggs
1 cup buttermilk
2 teaspoons vanilla
5 cups flour

1 teaspoon baking soda
1 teaspoon baking powder
¾ teaspoon salt
3 cups fresh or frozen
   blueberries
Sugar for topping (optional)

In a mixing bowl, cream butter and sugar. Add eggs, buttermilk, and vanilla. Mix well. In another bowl, combine flour, baking soda, baking powder, and salt. Stir into creamed mixture just until moistened. Fold in blueberries. Batter will be thick. Fill greased or paper-lined miniature muffin cups with about 1 tablespoon batter. Sprinkle with sugar if desired. Bake at 400 degrees for 10 to 15 minutes or until muffins test done. Cool for 5 minutes before removing from pan to a wire rack. Yield: 7 dozen.

Mrs. Reuben (Martha) Byler, Atlantic, PA

Glazed Zucchini Bread

3 eggs, beaten
1¼ cups sugar
1 tablespoon vanilla
1 cup oil
2 cups flour
¾ tablespoon cinnamon

1 teaspoon salt
2 teaspoons baking soda
¼ teaspoon baking powder
¼ teaspoon nutmeg
2 cups grated zucchini
1 cup chopped nuts

In a mixing bowl, beat together eggs, sugar, and vanilla. Stir in oil. Add flour, cinnamon, salt, baking soda, baking powder, and nutmeg. Mix well. Add zucchini and nuts. Pour into greased and floured pans. Bake at 350 degrees for 1 hour (if using glass pans, bake at 300 degrees for 1 hour). Glaze while still hot.

Glaze:

1 to 2 tablespoons
   melted butter
½ cup powdered sugar

¼ teaspoon vanilla
¼ teaspoon almond flavoring
Dash salt

Combine all. If you want it to soak into bread, make it very thin. Immediately after removing bread from oven, poke small holes in top and pour glaze over it.

Tip: If you don't want to glaze your bread, increase sugar in batter to 2 cups.

Joann Miller, Fredericktown, OH

T-B-T Breakfast Sandwich

2 slices bacon, fried
1 egg, fried
1 slice tomato

2 slices bread, toasted
Salad dressing or
   mayonnaise (optional)

Place bacon, egg, and tomato on top of 1 slice of toast. Slather other slice of toast with salad dressing if desired. Place on top of tomato.

"A quick grab-and-go summer breakfast that is best when the tomatoes are ripe."

Anna Byler, Spartansburg, PA

Spinach and Tomato French Toast

3 eggs
Salt and pepper to taste
8 slices bread

4 cups torn fresh spinach
2 tomatoes, sliced
Shaved Parmesan cheese

In a bowl, beat eggs with salt and pepper. Dip bread slices in egg and place in a lightly greased skillet over medium heat. Cook one side until lightly browned. Place spinach, tomato slice, and cheese on each slice, pressing lightly to secure. Carefully flip and cook until done. Flip back over onto plate and serve open-faced.

Esther M. Peachey, Flemingsburg, KY

Corn-y Scrambled Eggs

1 to 3 cobs corn, cooked
1 onion, sliced
2 tablespoons butter
6 eggs
½ cup half and half

¾ teaspoon salt
¼ teaspoon garlic powder
⅛ teaspoon pepper
Cheese

Cut corn from cob with a sharp knife. Set aside. In a skillet, fry onions in butter until tender crisp. Add corn. In a bowl, beat eggs with half and half, salt, garlic powder, and pepper. Pour over onions and corn. Fry until eggs set. Add cheese to your desire. You can also add cooked bacon, sausage, or hot dogs.

Kathryn Troyer, Rutherford, TN

WATERMELON BOAT

1 large watermelon
1 honeydew melon, cut
  into cubes or balls
1 cantaloupe, cut into
  cubes or balls

2 pints fresh strawberries,
  hulled and halved
½ pound grapes

For watermelon boat: With a sharp knife, cut thin slice from bottom of melon for a level base. About 2 inches above center of melon, mark a horizontal cutting line with your knife. Cut into melon using line to guide you and making sure to cut all the way through melon. Gently pull off top section. Remove fruit from both sections, cutting watermelon into cubes or balls and leaving rind intact. To cut a decorative edge, place melon on its side. Position a 2½-inch 8-point star cookie cutter along the edge, allowing only half of the star to cut through rind. Cut all the way around until edge is complete. Combine fruits and spoon into melon boat. Serve with dip on the side.

DIP:

1 cup pineapple juice
1 cup sugar
2 teaspoons flour

2 eggs, beaten
1 cup heavy cream, whipped

In a saucepan, combine juice, sugar, and flour. Bring to a boil. Reduce heat to low. Stir one-quarter of mixture into beaten eggs until combined. Return all to saucepan. Cook, stirring, for 15 minutes, but do not boil. Cool. Fold in whipped cream.

LEAH RENAE MILLER, Millersburg, OH

Tip: Save and dry melon seeds. Mix into your birdseed, and your feathered friends will love you for it.

LYDIA MILLER, Loudonville, OH

Melon Summer Salad

1 cup watermelon balls

1 cup cantaloupe or
   honeydew melon balls

Juice of 1 lemon

¼ cup honey

½ cup whipping cream,
   whipped stiff

Lettuce leaves for serving

Sprinkle fruit balls with lemon juice then drizzle with honey. Chill. Just before serving, fold in whipped cream. Serve on crisp lettuce.

Mrs. Joe J. Miller, Lakeview, MI

Frozen Fruit

6 cups or less sugar

4 cans frozen white grape juice concentrate

1 (46 ounce) can pineapple juice

1 gallon red grapes, halved

1 gallon fresh pineapple, chunked

Approximately 15 quarts peaches, sliced or cubed

Mix sugar, grape juice concentrate, and pineapple juice in 20-quart canner. Stir until sugar and concentrate dissolve. Add grapes and pineapple. Fill canner with peaches. Stir to combine. Fill plastic freezer containers, leaving room for expansion. Freeze.

"A great treat to have on hand for lunch buckets or for unexpected company."

ELIZABETH SHETLER, Brinkhaven, OH

EGG SALAD ON TOMATO

Hard-boiled eggs
Mayonnaise
Mustard

Salt
Tomatoes
Paprika

Tweak amount of ingredients to meet your family's needs. Peel eggs, and in a bowl, finely mash them. Mix in mayonnaise, mustard, and salt to your taste. Slice ripe tomatoes rather thickly. Lay a single layer on a plate or platter. Spoon egg mixture on top. Sprinkle with paprika for color. Serve. Refrigerate leftovers immediately.

"A great addition to a picnic!"

BETHANY MARTIN, Homer City, PA

TOMATO SANDWICH

Salad dressing
Sliced bread
Deli meat (optional)

Sliced tomato
Salt and pepper to taste

Spread salad dressing on a slice of bread. Top with your choice of meat. Then top with slice of tomato. Sprinkle with salt and pepper. Enjoy!

ROSANNA STUTZMAN, Colchester, IL

COOL GARDEN SALAD

Tomatoes
Onions
Cucumbers
Green peppers
Broccoli
½ cup warm water

¼ cup vinegar
¼ cup sugar
¼ teaspoon salt
1 tablespoon Italian
  seasoning

Dice tomatoes, onions, cucumbers, green peppers, and broccoli into a large bowl. Adjust amounts to your taste. In a small bowl, blend warm water, vinegar, sugar, salt, and Italian seasoning. Pour over vegetables and stir to coat.

MRS. BENJAMIN WICKEY, Monroe, IN

Poppy Seed Salad

1 head lettuce
1 cup shredded
  Parmesan cheese
½ cup sliced and toasted
  almonds or pecans

1 cup cherry tomatoes
½ cup fried and
  crumbled bacon
1 cup garlic croutons

In a bowl, toss salad ingredients together, or layer on a large platter. Serve with poppy seed dressing. For variation, use Fritos BBQ Twists instead of croutons.

Poppy Seed Dressing:

1 cup sugar
½ cup mayonnaise
½ cup vinegar
¼ cup lemon juice
1 teaspoon mustard

1 teaspoon salt
¼ teaspoon pepper
1 teaspoon onion powder
1½ cups olive oil
1 tablespoon poppy seeds

In a blender, mix sugar, mayonnaise, vinegar, lemon juice, mustard, salt, pepper, and onion powder. Slowly drizzle in olive oil while blending. When dressing is thick, stop blending. Stir in poppy seeds. Pour into glass jar. Chill before serving.

KATHRYN TROYER, Rutherford, TN

Fresh Corn Salad

8 ears fresh corn, husked and cleaned

½ cup vegetable oil

¼ cup apple cider vinegar

1½ teaspoons lemon juice

¼ cup minced fresh parsley

2 teaspoons sugar

1 teaspoon salt

½ teaspoon dried or 1 teaspoon fresh basil

⅛ teaspoon cayenne pepper

½ cup chopped onion

⅓ cup chopped green bell pepper

⅓ cup chopped red bell pepper

2 large tomatoes, seeded and chopped

In a large saucepan, cook corn in enough boiling water to cover it for 5 to 7 minutes or until tender. Drain, cool, and set aside. In a large bowl, mix oil, vinegar, lemon juice, parsley, sugar, salt, basil, and cayenne pepper. Cut cooled corn off cob. It should measure 4 cups. Add corn, onions, and peppers to mixture. Cover and chill several hours or overnight. Before serving, stir in tomatoes.

Mary Ellen Schwartz, Mayslick, KY

Broccoli Salad

1 head broccoli, chopped
10 slices bacon, fried
  and crumbled
1 cup shredded
  cheddar cheese
2 hard-boiled eggs, chopped

¼ cup sliced carrots
⅓ cup frozen peas
Cauliflower, chopped
  (optional)
Raisins (optional)

In a large bowl, combine broccoli, bacon, cheese, eggs, carrots, peas, cauliflower, and raisins.

DRESSING:

1 cup mayonnaise
⅓ cup sugar

2 tablespoons vinegar

Blend mayonnaise, sugar, and vinegar until smooth. When ready to eat, mix dressing into salad.

RUTH M. YODER, Berlin, PA

Overnight Cauliflower Salad

1 head lettuce
1 head cauliflower
1 package frozen peas
2 cups mayonnaise

1 package dry ranch
  dressing mix
1 package shredded cheese
½ pound bacon, fried
  and chopped

In a large bowl, tear lettuce into bite-size pieces. Chop cauliflower and layer over lettuce. Top with peas. Spread mayonnaise over top, covering all and sealing edges well. Sprinkle dressing mix over mayonnaise. Sprinkle with cheese and top with bacon. Put a lid on the bowl and refrigerate 24 hours. Mix well before serving.

Mrs. Rebecca Byler, Spartansburg, PA

Cucumbers in Dressing

1 cup mayonnaise
¼ cup sugar
¼ cup vinegar

¼ teaspoon salt
4 cups sliced cucumbers

In a bowl, mix mayonnaise, sugar, vinegar, and salt. Add cucumbers and stir to coat. Cover and refrigerate for 2 hours.

Mrs. Reuben (Martha) Byler, Atlantic, PA

Cucumber Salad

1 cup mayonnaise
¼ cup sugar
4 teaspoons vinegar
½ teaspoon dill weed
½ teaspoon salt

4 medium cucumbers,
  peeled and thinly sliced
½ medium onion, shredded,
  chopped, or sliced

In a bowl, combine mayonnaise, sugar, vinegar, dill weed, and salt. Mix well. Toss in cucumbers and onion. Cover and chill at least 1 hour.

"This is delicious served over cooked potatoes."
Ioana Joy Petersheim, Fredericktown, OH

Marinated Zucchini Salad

1 can tuna packed in water
1½ cups thinly sliced
   unpeeled zucchini
   or yellow squash
2 medium ripe tomatoes,
   sliced thinly
1 small red onion, sliced
½ lemon, sliced thinly

½ cup olive oil
2 tablespoons fresh
   lemon juice
½ teaspoon pepper
1 clove garlic, minced
2 cups salad greens, torn
   into bite-size pieces

In a large bowl, mix tuna, zucchini, tomatoes, red onion, and lemon slices. In a small bowl, mix oil, lemon juice, pepper, and garlic. Pour over tuna salad. Cover and refrigerate several hours. At serving time, place greens in a salad bowl, spoon marinated tuna salad on top, toss to mix well, and serve.

WANDA E. BRUNSTETTER

Harvard Beets

4 to 5 fresh beets
⅓ cup sugar
2 tablespoons flour
½ teaspoon salt

⅓ cup vinegar
¼ teaspoon minced onion
1 tablespoon butter

In a saucepan, cook beets; drain off liquid, reserving ⅔ cup. Dice beets. In a double boiler, combine sugar, flour, and salt. Add vinegar to beet juice and gradually stir into dry ingredients. Cook in double boiler, stirring constantly until smooth and thickened. Add beets and onion. If necessary, continue to cook up to 15 minutes to reheat beets. Stir in butter. Makes 6 to 8 servings.

MRS. LLOYD KUEFER, Kincardine, Ontario

Baked Cauliflower

1 medium onion, chopped
1 garlic clove, minced
4 tablespoons butter, divided
2 tablespoons olive oil
1 (16 ounce) package fresh
  or frozen cauliflower

1 teaspoon salt
½ teaspoon pepper
⅛ teaspoon nutmeg
¼ cup dry breadcrumbs
¼ cup shredded cheese

In a large skillet, sauté onion and garlic in 2 tablespoons of the butter and olive oil until onion is tender. Add cauliflower, salt, pepper, and nutmeg. Sauté for 2 minutes. Transfer to a greased 1-quart baking dish. Melt remaining 2 tablespoons butter and toss with breadcrumbs. Sprinkle over cauliflower. Cover and bake at 350 degrees for 15 minutes. Uncover and bake 10 minutes or until heated through. Sprinkle with cheese and bake 3 to 5 minutes until cheese is melted.

Mrs. Reuben (Martha) Byler, Atlantic, PA

GREEN BEAN SPECIALTY

1 small onion, sliced
1 clove garlic, sliced
2 carrots, sliced
2 tablespoons butter
2 tablespoons olive oil

2 to 3 pounds green beans,
   trimmed and cut
Salt and pepper to taste
Fresh herbs to taste
   (chive, parsley, etc.)
2 tablespoons sour cream

In a large skillet, sauté onion, garlic, and carrot in butter and olive oil. Add beans, stirring often until vegetables are almost soft. Season to taste with salt and pepper and fresh herbs. Cover and steam until ready to serve. Stir in sour cream right before serving.

MARY ELLEN SCHWARTZ, Mayslick, KY

PACIFIC GREEN BEANS

1 pound fresh green beans
1 small onion, finely chopped
1 tablespoon margarine,
   butter, or bacon fat
¼ cup water
¼ teaspoon salt

2 teaspoons chopped fresh
   or 2 teaspoons dried
   summer savory leaves
1 tablespoon chopped
   fresh parsley

Cut beans in 1½-inch pieces or leave whole but trimmed. In a 3-quart saucepan, cook onion in margarine over medium heat, stirring frequently until onion is tender. Stir in beans, water, and salt. Heat to boiling; reduce heat. Cover and simmer, stirring occasionally, until beans are crisp-tender (10 to 13 minutes for pieces or 13 to 16 minutes for whole beans). Stir in savory and parsley.

MRS. LIZZIE SCHWARTZ, Geneva, IN

CASHEW GREEN BEANS

1 gallon green beans,
    trimmed and cut
1 cup butter

1½ cups sliced cashews
1 cup honey

In a pot, cover beans with water and cook. Meanwhile, brown the butter in a skillet. Add cashews and stir. Add honey last. Remove from heat. Drain water from tender cooked beans and add cashew mixture. Stir well and serve.

ANNA MILLER, Loudonville, OH

EGGPLANT CASSEROLE

2 cups cubed eggplant
2 tablespoons butter
1 tablespoon diced onion
½ teaspoon salt
⅛ teaspoon pepper

¼ teaspoon dry mustard
2 tablespoons flour
1 cup milk
1½ cups shredded
    cheese, divided

In a saucepan, cook eggplant until tender. In another saucepan, melt butter. Add onion, salt, pepper, mustard, and flour. Stir over medium heat for 2 minutes. Add milk and cook, stirring until sauce thickens. Stir in 1 cup of cheese. Stir over low heat until cheese is melted. Place eggplant cubes in a baking dish and pour sauce over eggplant. Cover with remaining ½ cup cheese. Bake uncovered at 350 degrees for 30 minutes.

SUSAN C. SCHWARTZ, Berne, IN

FRIED ZUCCHINI FRITTERS

2 cups grated zucchini
¼ cup flour
1 teaspoon salt
1 teaspoon baking powder

1 egg
1 cup shredded cheese
Butter

In a mixing bowl, mix zucchini, flour, salt, baking powder, egg, and cheese. Drop batter by spoonful into a well-buttered skillet. Fry over medium heat until golden brown on both sides.

SADIE GLICK, Howard, PA

Zucchini Fries

1 medium zucchini	1 egg, lightly beaten
½ cup flour	⅓ cup milk
1 teaspoon onion salt	1 teaspoon vegetable oil
1 teaspoon oregano	4 cups crushed corn flakes
½ teaspoon garlic powder	Oil for deep-frying

Cut zucchini in half lengthwise, remove seeds, and cut into 8 wedges. In a bowl, combine flour, onion salt, oregano, and garlic powder. In another bowl, mix egg, milk, and oil. Stir into dry mixture. Dip zucchini in batter then roll in corn flakes. Deep-fry in oil until lightly browned.

MRS. REUBEN (MARTHA) BYLER, Atlantic, PA

Broccoli Soup

2 cups diced potatoes
1 cup diced carrots
1 small onion, chopped
1 cup water
1 cup diced ham or bacon

1 cup chopped broccoli
4 cups milk, divided
½ cup flour
1 cup shredded cheese
Salt and pepper to taste

In a saucepan, cook potatoes, carrots, and onion with water until soft. Add ham, broccoli, and 2 cups of milk. Bring to a boil and simmer for a few minutes. In a gravy shaker or mason jar, blend flour and remaining 2 cups milk. Add to soup and return to boiling. You can add more milk if the soup is too thick. Add cheese and season with salt and pepper to taste. Serve.

Mary Ann Yutzy, Bloomfield, IA

Corn-Cheddar Chowder

3 tablespoons butter
1 onion, chopped
2½ cups boiling water
2 chicken bouillon cubes
6 potatoes, peeled and diced
2 tablespoons flour

3 cups half and half or
  rich milk, divided
2 cups fresh corn
2 cups shredded
  cheddar cheese
½ teaspoon celery salt
Salt and pepper to taste

In a heavy saucepan, melt butter, add onion, and sauté. Add boiling water and chicken bouillon cubes, stirring until cubes are dissolved. Add potatoes. Cook 15 minutes over low heat. In a small saucepan, mix flour with 1 cup of half and half; heat well. Add to hot mixture and stir until thickened. Add corn and remaining 2 cups half and half. Simmer for 10 minutes over low heat. Remove from heat. Add cheese, celery salt, salt, and pepper, stirring until fully combined. Serves 4 people.

"A hearty soup for a chilly fall harvest supper."
Kathryn Detweiler, West Farmington, OH

BURGER 'N' FRIES HAYSTACK

HAMBURGER MIXTURE:

2 pounds hamburger

2 eggs, beaten

⅔ cup quick oats

⅔ cup ketchup

1 tablespoon parsley

1 teaspoon seasoned salt

1 teaspoon pepper

1 teaspoon garlic powder

4 tablespoons brown sugar

⅔ cup water

2 small onions

In a bowl, combine hamburger, eggs, oats, ketchup, parsley, seasoned salt, pepper, garlic powder, brown sugar, and water. In a large skillet, brown hamburger, stirring to keep from clumping. When meat is brown, add onions. Serves 16 people.

HAYSTACK INGREDIENTS:

Hamburger mixture

½ loaf bread, toasted
   and cubed

French fries

Ketchup

Mustard

3 large tomatoes, diced

1 pint dill pickles, chopped

1 onion, chopped

¾ cup shredded cheese

2½ quarts cheese sauce

Put each ingredient in serving bowls. Have each person layer their own haystack on their plates.

"Makes a complete meal for a warm summer's eve."

RUBY BORNTRAGER, Goshen, IN

CHICKEN PESTO WITH ZOODLES

12 ounces chicken breast
2 zucchini
2 cups pesto sauce

1 cup peas
1 cup cherry tomatoes, halved

In a skillet, sear chicken for 5 to 7 minutes. Turn chicken over. Cover with lid and cook 10 to 12 minutes over medium-low heat. While chicken cooks, use matchstick setting on a mandoline to slice zucchini lengthwise into zoodles. When chicken is done, remove from skillet. Cool and slice. Place zoodles and pesto in skillet, cooking 3 to 5 minutes until warm but not too soft. Add in peas, tomatoes, and chicken. Stir to combine. Serve immediately.

SARAH MILLER, Big Sandy, TN

CHICKEN AND VEGGIE STIR-FRY

Cooking oil
Chicken breast, diced
Carrots, sliced
Onions, diced
Vegetables of any amount and combination, sliced or

diced (cauliflower, yellow squash, zucchini, cabbage, green beans, asparagus, cherry tomatoes)
Soy sauce

In a large skillet, heat oil and fry chicken until tender. Add carrots and onions. Stir-fry until tender. Add other vegetables of choice. If using asparagus or cherry tomatoes, add at very end of cooking so they are not overcooked. When vegetables are tender, drizzle with soy sauce. Remove from heat and let stand a few minutes. Serve over rice and top with white sauce.

WHITE SAUCE:

1 cup mayonnaise
½ cup sour cream
¼ cup water
3 tablespoons sugar
1 tablespoon lemon juice

6 drops soy sauce
½ teaspoon garlic powder
½ teaspoon paprika
¼ teaspoon ground ginger

Mix all ingredients well.

MARY JOYCE PETERSHEIM, Fredericktown, OH

Eggplant Spaghetti

2 tablespoons olive
oil or butter
2 cups cubed eggplant
(½-inch cubes)
1 cup cubed summer squash
½ cup chopped onion
¼ to ½ cup chopped
bell pepper
⅓ cup chopped celery
2 to 3 cloves garlic, minced

2 cups diced fresh or
canned tomatoes
½ cup water
3 ounces spaghetti
noodles, broken
Basil to taste
Salt and pepper to taste
Herb salt to taste
1 to 2 cups shredded
mozzarella cheese

In a large pot or skillet, heat oil and sauté eggplant, squash, onion, bell pepper, celery, and garlic to tender. Add tomatoes and water and bring to boil. Add spaghetti and basil, salt, pepper, and herb salt to your taste. Return to boil. Cover pot and turn off heat. Let set until spaghetti is tender. Stir in cheese and allow to melt.

Mary Joyce Petersheim, Fredericktown, OH

Green Bean Meal

3 pounds chunked ham
Small, early potatoes
   with skins on

Fresh green beans, snapped

In an 8-quart kettle, put ham on bottom. Top with layer of potatoes then green beans. Fill the pot three-quarters full of water. Cook until tender.

"This is one of our favorite summer meals."

Anna Byler, Spartansburg, PA

Favorite Green Beans

1 pound ground beef
2 tablespoons chopped
   fresh garlic
½ cup chopped onion
2 to 3 pounds fresh green
   beans, snapped

1 teaspoon paprika
1 teaspoon salt
½ cup ketchup (optional)
4 ounces cream
   cheese (optional)

In a heavy saucepan, brown beef, garlic, and onion with lid on. Add green beans, paprika, and salt. Slowly simmer until beans reach desired tenderness. May need to add water. For a creamy zest, add ketchup and cream cheese.

Norma Yutzy, Drakesville, IA

Sausage Squash Skillet

1 pound sausage, sliced
3 tablespoons chopped onion
3 medium yellow
   squash, sliced

Seasoning of your choice
Cheddar cheese, shredded

In a skillet, fry sausage and onions until sausage is almost cooked through. Add squash and sauté until squash is soft, about 10 minutes. Season and sprinkle with cheese. Let melt before serving.

Norma Yutzy, Drakesville, IA

TOMATO PIE CASSEROLE

CRUST:

3 cups shredded
   unpeeled zucchini
1 cup baking mix or flour
½ teaspoon oregano

½ cup vegetable oil
3 eggs, beaten
¼ teaspoon salt
Pinch pepper

In a bowl, combine zucchini, baking mix, oregano, oil, eggs, salt, and pepper. Pour into a lightly greased 9x13-inch pan. Bake at 350 degrees for 20 minutes or until firm.

FILLING:

3 ripe tomatoes
1 pound hamburger,
   browned
½ teaspoon basil
½ teaspoon Italian seasoning
¼ teaspoon parsley

½ teaspoon oregano
¼ teaspoon garlic powder
¼ teaspoon pepper
Parmesan cheese
1 cup mayonnaise
8 ounces shredded cheese

Peel and slice tomatoes. Place a layer of half the tomatoes over crust. Spread on half of hamburger. Sprinkle with all the basil, Italian seasoning, parsley, oregano, garlic powder, and pepper. Sprinkle with Parmesan cheese. Repeat layers of tomatoes and hamburger. In a bowl, mix mayonnaise and shredded cheese. Spread over top. Bake at 350 degrees for 35 to 40 minutes until lightly browned.

RUTH M. YODER, Berlin, PA

Squash Skillet

1 pound ground beef
1 cup chopped onion
¾ cup chopped green
    bell pepper
1 clove garlic, minced
1½ teaspoons salt
¼ teaspoon pepper

1 teaspoon chili powder
5 cups coarsely shredded
    zucchini (do not peel)
2 tomatoes, diced
1¼ cups corn (fresh
    cut from cob)
2 cups tomato juice

In a large skillet, fry ground beef, onions, bell pepper, and garlic until done.
Add salt, pepper, chili powder, zucchini, tomatoes, corn, and tomato juice.
Simmer slowly for 30 minutes.

Kathryn Troyer, Rutherford, TN

ZUCCHINI BOATS

2 (10-inch long) zucchini
2 cups browned ground beef
1½ cups cooked rice
1 egg
2 tablespoons ketchup

2 teaspoons Italian seasoning
⅓ cup chopped onion
¾ cup pizza sauce
Sea salt and pepper to taste
½ cup mozzarella cheese

Cut zucchini in half lengthwise. Place on cookie sheet and bake at 350 degrees for 20 minutes. Cool slightly and scoop out seed cavity. Turn upside down to drain. In a bowl, mix beef, rice, egg, ketchup, Italian seasoning, onion, pizza sauce, and salt and pepper to taste. Divide mixture into each cavity. Sprinkle with cheese. Bake for 30 minutes.

IOANA JOY PETERSHEIM, Fredericktown, OH

ZUCCHINI CASSEROLE

3 cups shredded
  unpeeled zucchini
1 quart pizza or
  spaghetti sauce

1 pound ground
  beef, browned
¾ cup shredded cheese
1 cup broken uncooked
  spaghetti

Mix all together in a casserole dish. Bake at 350 degrees for 1 hour.

FREDA FISHER, Leola, PA

Black Raspberry Tapioca

3 quarts black
   raspberry juice
2 cups fine pearl tapioca
2 cups sugar
¾ cup raspberry gelatin or
   1 pack berry-flavored
   drink mix

1 (16 ounce) container
   whipped topping
4 (8 ounce) packages cream
   cheese, softened

In a pot, heat berry juice to boiling and add tapioca. Cook until clear then add sugar and gelatin. Cool. In a large bowl, mix whipped topping and cream cheese. Stir into cooled tapioca mixture. Pour into serving dish. Chill.

Mrs. Lizzie Schwartz, Geneva, IN

Molded French Cream

Oil
1 cup sour cream
1 cup heavy whipping cream
¾ cup sugar
1 tablespoon unflavored
   gelatin

¼ cup water
1 (8 ounce) package cream
   cheese, softened
½ teaspoon vanilla
2 to 3 quarts fruit

Brush a 4-cup mold with oil. Combine sour cream and heavy whipping cream in a saucepan. Beat in sugar. Place over a very low heat until sugar is dissolved. In a bowl, sprinkle gelatin over water to dissolve. Stir into warm cream mixture. Remove from heat. In a mixing bowl, beat cream cheese until light and fluffy. Gradually add sour cream mixture and vanilla. Beat thoroughly until smooth. Pour into mold and chill. Serve on a platter with fruit. The longer it sets, the smoother and richer it gets.

"Perfect to serve with summertime fruits."

Mary Ellen Miller, Apple Creek, OH

ELDERBERRY PIE

1¾ cups elderberries
1¾ cups water, divided
1 cup sugar
2 teaspoons lemon juice
¼ cup Clear Jel

1 (9 inch) unbaked pie
 shell and top
1 tablespoon heavy cream
1 to 2 tablespoons sugar

In a saucepan, bring elderberries and ¾ cup water to a boil. Add 1 cup sugar and lemon juice. In a bowl, mix remaining 1 cup water and Clear Jel. Slowly add mixture to boiling elderberries, stirring until thickened and clear. Remove from heat. Pour into pie shell. Add top crust and seal. Brush top crust with cream and sprinkle with 1 to 2 tablespoons sugar. Bake at 400 degrees for 10 minutes, then reduce heat to 300 degrees and bake 30 minutes.

"This is my husband's favorite pie."

MARY JOYCE PETERSHEIM, Fredericktown, OH

BLUEBERRY BUCKLE

¼ cup vegetable oil
¾ teaspoon salt
1 egg
¾ cup sugar
¾ cup milk

1 teaspoon vanilla
2 cups flour
2½ teaspoons baking powder
2 cups blueberries
1 tablespoon flour

In a mixing bowl, combine oil, salt, egg, sugar, milk, and vanilla; beat well. Add flour and baking powder. Toss blueberries with 1 tablespoon flour then fold into batter. Pour into greased 9x9-inch baking dish.

CRUMBS:

½ cup sugar
¼ cup butter, softened

½ teaspoon cinnamon
½ cup flour

In a small bowl, mix sugar, butter, cinnamon, and flour until crumbly, then sprinkle on top of batter. Bake at 350 degrees for 45 minutes.

MARY BONTRAGER, Middlebury, IN

BLUEBERRY SUPREME PIE

¾ cup maple syrup
2 teaspoons cornstarch
1 cup water

3 cups blueberries, divided
Cinnamon
1 baked pie shell

In a saucepan, cook maple syrup, cornstarch, water, and 1 cup blueberries. Cook until thickened. Remove from heat. Add remaining 2 cups blueberries and a little cinnamon to taste. Pour into pie shell. Let cool to room temperature before serving.

CEVILLA GINGERICH, Dundee, OH

Gooseberry Cream

3 cups gooseberries
½ cup sugar
½ cup heavy cream,
   well chilled

¼ cup crème fraîche (or sour
   cream, cream cheese,
   or ricotta cheese)
¼ cup sugar

Remove tops and tails of gooseberries using scissors. Cut berries lengthwise. In a heavy saucepan, cook berries with ½ cup sugar over moderate heat, stirring occasionally, until liquid is thickened (about 5 minutes). Simmer while mashing berries with a fork to a coarse puree (about 2 minutes). Chill for about 1 hour.

In a bowl, beat the heavy cream with crème fraîche until it holds soft peaks. Add ¼ cup sugar and beat again until it holds soft peaks. Fold the chilled puree into the creamed mixture until well combined.

It may be made 3 hours ahead of serving, covered, and refrigerated.

LENA TROYER, Redding, IA

Coconut Peach Dessert

1⅓ cups flaked coconut
½ cup chopped almonds
⅓ cup sugar
2 tablespoons flour

⅛ teaspoon salt
2 egg whites, lightly beaten
½ teaspoon almond extract

In a bowl, combine coconut, almonds, sugar, flour, and salt. Add egg whites and almond extract. Line a baking sheet with foil and grease foil well. Spread coconut mixture into a 9-inch circle on foil. Bake at 325 degrees for 20 to 25 minutes or until lightly browned. Cool on a wire rack. Refrigerate.

TOPPING:
2 cups whipped topping
4 cups sliced fresh or frozen peaches
½ cup sugar

Place crust on serving plate. Spread with whipped topping. Combine peaches and sugar. Spoon over whipped topping. Cut into wedges. Serve immediately.

JUDITH MILLER, Fredericktown, OH

PEACHES AND CREAM SUPREME

CRUST:

1 cup flour	½ cup butter
⅔ cup sugar	1 teaspoon peach syrup
1 teaspoon baking powder	1 teaspoon vanilla
¼ teaspoon salt	2 eggs

In a bowl, mix all ingredients. Spread evenly in a greased 10-inch pie pan.

FILLING:

⅓ cup sugar	3 ounces cream cheese
¼ cup sour cream	1 egg
½ teaspoon salt	

In a bowl, blend sugar, sour cream, salt, cream cheese, and egg. Pour over crust. Bake at 350 degrees for 20 to 25 minutes.

TOPPING:

Peaches	¼ cup brown sugar
1 cup sour cream	

Slice as many peaches as you wish and layer on top while crust is hot. In a bowl, blend sour cream and brown sugar. Pour over peaches and bake 5 minutes.

DORCAS MARIE YODER, Meyersdale, PA

PEACH CREAM PIE

4 cups sliced fresh peaches
1 cup sugar, divided
2 tablespoons flour
1 egg

¼ teaspoon salt
½ teaspoon vanilla
1 cup sour cream
2 unbaked pie shells

In a bowl, place peaches and sprinkle with ¼ cup of sugar. Let stand several minutes. Add remaining ¾ cup sugar, flour, egg, salt, and vanilla. Fold in sour cream. Pour into pie shells. Sprinkle with topping. Bake at 375 degrees for 25 minutes until set.

TOPPING:

⅓ cup sugar
⅓ cup flour

¼ cup butter
1 teaspoon cinnamon

Mix until crumbly.

LIZ MILLER, Decatur, IN

PINEAPPLE SPONGE PIE

2 eggs, separated
1 cup sugar
1 tablespoon cornstarch
2 cups crushed or grated
    pineapple, drained

2 tablespoons melted butter
⅓ teaspoon lemon juice
1 (9 inch) unbaked pie shell

In a mixing bowl, beat egg yolks, sugar, and cornstarch together. Add pineapple, butter, and lemon juice. In another bowl, beat egg whites to stiff peaks. Fold into first mixture. Pour into pie shell. Bake at 400 degrees for 10 minutes until top starts to brown and puff up. Reduce oven temperature to 325 degrees and bake 25 to 30 minutes. Cool before serving.

MRS. BENJAMIN WICKEY, Monroe, IN

Green Tomato Pie

4 to 5 green tomatoes	1 teaspoon cinnamon
¾ cup sugar	4 tablespoons vinegar
¾ cup brown sugar	1 unbaked pie shell and top
2 tablespoons flour	1 tablespoon butter

Thinly slice tomatoes and remove as many seeds as possible. In a large bowl, mix sugar, brown sugar, flour, and cinnamon. Add green tomatoes and vinegar and gently toss to coat. Put in pie shell. Dot with butter. Add top crust. Bake at 350 degrees for 1 hour.

"Tastes like apple pie."
BETTY BYLER, Smicksburg, PA

Green Tomato Cake

2 cups sugar	1 tablespoon cinnamon
1 cup lard	1½ teaspoons nutmeg
3 eggs	1 cup chopped nuts
1 tablespoon vanilla	1 cup raisins
3 cups flour	2½ cups grated green
1 teaspoon salt	tomatoes
1 tablespoon baking soda	¼ to ½ cup shredded coconut

In a mixing bowl, cream sugar, lard, eggs, and vanilla. Add flour, salt, baking soda, cinnamon, and nutmeg. Mix well. Add nuts, raisins, and green tomatoes. Pour into greased 9x13-inch pan. Sprinkle with coconut. Bake at 350 degrees for 1 hour or until it tests done.

*"A delicious way to use the late green tomatoes
during summer or after first frost hits."*
MRS. LEVI MILLER, Junction City, OH

CHOCOLATE ZUCCHINI BROWNIES

4 eggs
1½ cups oil
2 cups sugar
2 cups flour
2 teaspoons baking soda

1 teaspoon cinnamon
1 teaspoon salt
4 tablespoons cocoa powder
1 teaspoon vanilla
3 cups grated zucchini

Mix all ingredients. Spread into a greased 9x13-inch pan. Bake at 350 degrees for 25 to 30 minutes. When cool, spread with cream cheese icing.

CREAM CHEESE ICING:

3 ounces cream
  cheese, softened
½ cup butter, softened

2 cups powdered sugar
2 tablespoons cocoa powder
1 teaspoon vanilla

Blend together cream cheese and butter. Add powdered sugar and cocoa powder. Add vanilla. Beat until smooth.

BETTY BYLER, Smicksburg, PA

ZUCCHINI CHOCOLATE COFFEE CAKE

2 cups shredded zucchini
1¼ cups sugar
½ cup vegetable oil
1 egg
2 teaspoons vanilla

2 cups flour
½ cup cocoa powder
1 teaspoon salt
1 teaspoon baking soda

In a mixing bowl, combine zucchini, sugar, oil, egg, and vanilla. Add flour, cocoa powder, salt, and baking soda. Mix well. Pour into a greased 9x13-inch pan. Bake at 350 degrees for 20 minutes. Cool.

FROSTING:

1 heaping teaspoon
  instant coffee
¼ cup hot water
2 cups powdered sugar

¼ cup cocoa powder
¼ cup butter, softened
Milk

In mixing bowl, dissolve instant coffee in hot water. Add powdered sugar, cocoa powder, and butter. Beat well. Add milk a tablespoon at a time to reach desired consistency. Spread on cooled cake.

FREDA FISHER, Leola, PA

Zucchini Squash Cake

1 cup peeled and
   grated zucchini
2 cups sugar
4 eggs
1½ cups corn oil
3 cups flour

2 teaspoons baking powder
1 teaspoon baking soda
1 teaspoon cinnamon
½ teaspoon salt
1 cup chopped nuts or raisins
1 teaspoon vanilla

In a large mixing bowl, combine zucchini, sugar, eggs, and oil. Add flour, baking powder, baking soda, cinnamon, and salt. Mix well. Stir in nuts or raisins and vanilla. Pour into greased 9x13-inch pan. Bake at 350 degrees for 40 to 45 minutes.

REBECCA GIROD, Berne, IN

Zucchini Pie

3 cups peeled and
   shredded zucchini
1 cup sugar
3 tablespoons flour
1 teaspoon cinnamon

1 teaspoon lemon juice
Pat softened butter
1 (9 inch) unbaked pie
   shell with top

In a mixing bowl, mix zucchini, sugar, flour, cinnamon, lemon juice, and butter. Pour into pie shell. Cover with crust, seal, and vent. Bake at 350 degrees for 45 minutes.

MRS. DAVID KURTZ, Smicksburg, PA

BLACKBERRY JELLY

Blackberries
Perma Flo

Sugar

In a large saucepan, cover blackberries with water and bring to a boil. Boil for 15 to 20 minutes. Remove from heat, put through a cloth, and squeeze out all the juice. For every 4 cups juice, add ¾ cup Perma Flo and 4 cups sugar. Keep stirring until it thickens. Pour into jelly jars. To seal jars, cold-pack in water bath for 8 minutes.

MRS. DAVID KURTZ, Smicksburg, PA

ELDERBERRY JELLY

9 cups elderberry juice
1½ cups Sure-Jell

¾ cup lemon juice
13½ cups sugar

In a stockpot, bring juice, Sure-Jell, and lemon juice to a boil. Add sugar. Bring to rapid boil that can't be stirred down. Boil for 10 minutes. Cool slightly. Pour into prepared jars. To seal jars, cold-pack for 10 minutes.

MRS. REUBEN (MARTHA) BYLER, Atlantic, PA

PEACH MARMALADE

5 cups mashed peaches
7 cups sugar
2 cups crushed pineapple

1 (6 ounce) package gelatin (peach, apricot, orange, or raspberry)

In a stockpot, combine peaches, sugar, and pineapple. Boil for 15 minutes. Add gelatin and stir until dissolved. Pour into containers. Cool; freeze or seal.

LINDA FISHER, Leola, PA

PEACH JAM

6 cups crushed peaches
5 cups sugar

1 large box peach gelatin
(or 1 small box each of
peach and apricot)

In a stockpot, mix peaches and sugar. Let stand 6 hours. You can use fresh fruit powder to preserve color. Bring to a boil. Boil 5 minutes. Take off stove and add gelatin. Store in jars in refrigerator or cold pack to seal jars. It is a basic recipe that can be used with most any fruit.

RACHEL KUEFER, Kincardine, Ontario

Canning Peaches and Pears Tip

When canning peaches, I use full-strength pineapple juice instead of a sugary syrup. When canning pears, I use half pineapple juice and half water.

MARYANN KEMPF, Winterset, IA

Beets Tip

When you are cooking a large pot of red beets to can, it doesn't need to cook and sputter, making a big mess on your kitchen stove. Instead, cook your pot of beets in the evening on medium heat with a lid on for 10 minutes. Turn off the heat and leave the lid on. Let it sit overnight until next morning. The beets will be soft, cooled, and ready to peel and can. Remember to strain some of the red beet water to use in your recipes for canning beets for lovely red coloring.

RUTH M. YODER, Berlin, PA

PICKLED RED BEETS

3 cups sugar
1 heaping tablespoon salt

1 cup beet water
1 cup vinegar

In a stockpot, cook beets until tender, drain (reserving beet water), peel, and cut. In a saucepan, bring sugar, salt, beet water, and vinegar to a boil. Divide into 4 quart jars. Add beets, then add beet water to fill jars. Cold-pack in hot water bath for 10 to 15 minutes to seal.

"In the spring at Easter, when we dye eggs, we like to put hard-boiled eggs in pickled beet juice for a day or two."

RUTHIE MILLER, Loudonville, OH

CANNING SWEET CORN IN 1 QUART

1 tablespoon sugar
1 teaspoon salt
⅛ teaspoon citric acid

Corn
Water

Put sugar, salt, and citric acid in jar and shake well to combine. Add a little water and shake again. Fill jars with fresh corn cut from the cob. Add water to fill jar. Pressure-can at 15 pounds pressure for 8 minutes.

BERTHA SCHWARTZ, Geneva, IN

PICKLED CORN

4 cups vinegar
1 cup sugar
1 tablespoon salt
8 cups fresh corn
  (about 12 ears)

½ head cabbage,
  finely chopped
2 red bell peppers,
  finely chopped
1 tablespoon celery seed
1 tablespoon mustard seed

In a large kettle, combine vinegar, sugar, salt, and corn; bring to a boil. Add cabbage, bell peppers, celery seed, and mustard seed; bring to a boil again and cook a little longer. Pour into jars and seal in a hot water bath for 15 minutes.

LYDIA SCHWARTZ, New Auburn, WI

DILLY BEANS

2 pounds small tender
  green beans
1 teaspoon ground red
  pepper (optional), divided
4 cloves garlic

4 large heads dill
2 cups water
¼ cup pickling salt
2 cups vinegar

Trim ends of green beans and pack uniformly into 4 hot, sterile pint jars. To each pint, add ¼ teaspoon red pepper, 1 clove garlic, and 1 head dill. In a saucepan, bring water, salt, and vinegar to boil. Pour over beans. Add hot water if needed to cover beans within 1 inch of top rim. Seal jars with 2-piece lids and process 10 minutes in boiling water bath.

KARI DANETTE PETERSHEIM, Fredericktown, OH

Favorite Sweet Dill Pickles

Cucumbers, sliced
  ½-inch thick
6 cloves garlic
6 heads dill
6 pinches alum (optional)

2 cups vinegar
2 cups water
2 cups sugar
2 tablespoons salt
2 tablespoons turmeric

Fill 6 pint jars with cucumbers. Add 1 clove garlic, 1 head dill, and a pinch of alum (if using) in each jar. In a kettle, heat vinegar, water, sugar, salt, and turmeric to a boil. Pour hot brine over cucumbers. Put on lids. Seal in a water bath. Bring to a boil and let jars stand in hot water for 5 minutes.

Mrs. Amanda Byler, Curwensville, PA

Anna Troyer, Smicksburg, PA

Good Church Pickles

1¾ cups vinegar
3 cups water
2½ teaspoons salt
3½ cups sugar

1½ teaspoons turmeric
1½ teaspoons dry mustard
Cucumbers

In a stockpot, combine vinegar, water, salt, sugar, turmeric, and mustard. Bring to a boil. Stir to be sure sugar dissolves. Wash cucumbers and run them through a crinkle cutter or slicer. Fill jars with cucumbers. Pour pickling brine over them, making sure all air is out. Seal with 2-piece lids and cold-pack for 10 minutes. Enough brine for 7 pints.

Clara Yoder, Sugar Grove, PA

Marinara Sauce

8 stalks celery
9 onions
4 green bell peppers
9 quarts tomato juice, divided
3 tablespoons chili powder
6 tablespoons sea salt
9 tablespoons parsley flakes
6 tablespoons paprika

2 cups xylitol or other sweetener
3 tiny spoons stevia powder
1 quart sugar-free ketchup
2 cups Parmesan cheese
3 tablespoons oregano
3 tablespoons ground mustard
3 tablespoons pepper
1 gallon tomato paste

In a large stockpot, cook celery, onions, and bell peppers with 1 gallon tomato juice until soft. Run through blender. Add all remaining ingredients. Bring to rolling boil. Put in quart jars with 2-part lids. Cold-pack 10 to 15 minutes.

Norma Yutzy, Drakesville, IA

SALSA (TO CAN)

14 cups chopped tomatoes
3 cups chopped onions
2 cups chopped green
   bell peppers
½ cup diced hot
   peppers (optional)
½ cup tomato sauce
3 tablespoons salt

1 tablespoon chili powder
1 tablespoon garlic salt
½ teaspoon cumin
2 tablespoons sugar
5 tablespoons Therm Flo
½ cup vinegar

Chop vegetables the same size and shape. Do not cook vegetables. In a large stockpot, combine tomatoes, onions, bell peppers, and hot peppers. Add tomato sauce, salt, chili powder, garlic salt, cumin, and sugar. Mix the Therm Flo with the vinegar and pour over top. Mix well, pour into jars, and seal in a hot water bath for 15 minutes.

"It's the easiest salsa recipe I ever had. Amazing, easy, and delicious! Don't have to cook any vegetables beforehand."

LYDIA MILLER, Loudonville, OH

Pesto

½ cup nuts
2 cups packed basil and/or
   parsley, stems removed
1 to 2 cloves garlic

½ cup grated
   Parmesan cheese
Olive oil

Chop nuts in blender. Add basil, garlic, and cheese. Add enough olive oil to blend well.

ANNA M. BYLER, Commodore, PA

Freezing Vegetables

Clean and cut vegetables. Cover the bottom of a large skillet with water. Add vegetables until approximately half full. Cover with heavy lid. Cook on high, stirring once or twice. When vegetables obtain a bright green color, they are done. Drain. Pour into a cake pan to cool. Do not rinse away precious vitamins by cooling with water. When cool, package and freeze.

This works well for broccoli, cauliflower, and green beans, though green beans take a minute or two longer to cook.

Tip: Adding chicken base to your mixed vegetables will help color stay bright. Adding butter causes color to fade.

LEAH RENAE MILLER, Millersburg, OH

Tip: To keep color in cooked vegetables, add pinch of baking soda to the cooking water.

KARI DANETTE PETERSHEIM, Fredericktown, OH

Zucchini Relish

10 cups ground zucchini
4 cups chopped onion
5 teaspoons salt
3 cups sugar
2¼ cups vinegar
1 teaspoon dry mustard

1 teaspoon turmeric
1 teaspoon nutmeg (optional)
½ teaspoon pepper
2 cups flour
1 to 2 bell peppers, chopped

In a large container, combine zucchini, onion, and salt. Let stand overnight. In the morning, drain and save some of the brine. Rinse zucchini with cold water. In a bowl, combine sugar, vinegar, mustard, turmeric, nutmeg, and pepper. In a large pot, mix seasonings into zucchini. In a bowl, mix a little brine water into the flour to make a paste. Pour over zucchini and cook for 30 minutes. During the last 15 minutes of cooking, add bell peppers. Pour into jars and seal in a water bath for 5 minutes.

NATHAN AND ANNA FISHER, Salisbury, PA

Zucchini Pie Filling

20 cups water
15 cups shredded zucchini
2 (20 ounce) cans
    crushed pineapple
3 cups Perma Flo

5 cups sugar
1 cup water
1½ teaspoons salt
4 cups gelatin in
    flavor of choice

In a stockpot, boil 20 cups water. Add zucchini and pineapple; return to a boil. In a bowl, mix Perma Flo, sugar, and 1 cup water. Add this to zucchini. Cook until thick. Add salt and gelatin. Put into quart jars and seal in water bath for 15 to 20 minutes. We use this like tapioca. Open a jar and mix with whipped topping.

BERTHA SCHWARTZ, Geneva, IN

Zucchini Pineapple

4 quarts diced zucchini
1½ cups lemon juice

1 (46 ounce) can
    pineapple juice
4 cups sugar

Combine everything in a stockpot. Simmer for 20 minutes, stirring frequently. Pour into canning jars. Seal in water bath for no longer than 5 minutes.

"Tastes like pineapple, and a nice way to use up zucchini."

KATURAH MILLER, Loudonville, OH

BLUEBERRY PIE FILLING (TO CAN)

3½ quarts water
5 cups sugar
1 teaspoon salt
2¾ cups Perma Flo
   (not Clear Jel)

2 tablespoons lemon juice
5 quarts fresh blueberries

In a stockpot, bring water, sugar, and salt to a boil. In a bowl, mix Perma Flo with a little water to make thin paste. Add to boiling water and cook until thick. Add lemon juice. Place blueberries in a large bowl, pour boiling mixture over them, and stir gently. Put into sterile quart jars leaving plenty of head room. Fix lids. Seal by cold-packing in boiling water for 10 minutes. Let set in canner off heat for 15 minutes before removing. Great for pies, yogurt, waffles, fry pies, etc.

LINDA BURKHOLDER, Fresno, OH

FRUIT PIE FILLING

4 cups fresh or frozen
   fruit (cherries, black
   raspberries, or peaches)
4 cups water, divided

Dash lemon juice
2 cups sugar
½ cup Therm Flo

Place fruit in deep saucepan. Add 3½ cups water and lemon juice. Bring to a boil. In a bowl, mix sugar and Therm Flo with remaining ½ cup water. Add to fruit and return to boil. Remove from heat.

Note: Red food coloring can be added to cherries for coloring. To peaches, add ¼ cup peach or orange gelatin in place of lemon juice.

MARY ELLEN SCHWARTZ, Mayslick, KY

Elderberry Syrup

*When the elderberries are ripening, it's time to
think of winter cold and flu prevention.*

½ cup fresh elderberries,
   cleaned (or ¾ cup frozen)*

3 cups water

2 tablespoons grated
   ginger root

1 teaspoon whole cloves

1 to 2 cinnamon sticks

1 cup raw honey or 1¼ to 1½
   cups pure maple syrup

In a saucepan, bring berries, water, ginger, cloves, and cinnamon to a boil. Simmer for 30 to 45 minutes. Cool slightly. Mash berries. (They can be strained out of the juice.) Add honey.

Use the syrup within 3 to 4 weeks for a daily immune booster. Adults take 1 tablespoon daily. Children take 1 teaspoon daily. If you have the flu, take 1 dose every 2 to 3 hours.

*If using canned elderberries, use 1 quart in place of fresh berries and no water.

KATIE MILLER, Apple Creek, OH

Elderberry Gummies

1 cup elderberry
   syrup, divided

¼ cup plain gelatin powder

½ cup hot but not
   boiling water

1 tablespoon coconut oil

Place ¼ cup of warmed elderberry syrup in a 2-cup measuring cup and quickly whisk in gelatin. Add hot water and stir until smooth. Add remaining ¾ cup elderberry syrup. Grease glass pan or candy molds with coconut oil and pour in the syrup. Refrigerate 2 hours. Cut into pieces and store in a cool place.

"Very good for children when having a cold or flu."

KATIE MILLER, Apple Creek, OH

Garden Tips

Hummingbird Feed

1 cup sugar　　　　　　　　　4 cups water

In a saucepan, combine sugar and water and gently boil until sugar dissolves. Cool.

Warning: Never use honey because it is fatal to the birds. Food coloring is also not good for them.

Feenie Beiler, Delta, PA

Add Mint to Your Garden

Mint has many uses. Chew a sprig for fresh-smelling breath. Use leaves to make a tea to ease stomach pain, nausea, vomiting, and gas. Very soothing for whatever ails you.

Leah Yoder, Glenville, PA

Peppers and Tomatoes

Grow your peppers and tomatoes bigger and tastier by recycling eggshells. Soak crushed eggshells in water for 24 hours. Use the water on your plants to energize them.

Esther Miller, Rossiter, PA

Pesky Rabbits

To keep rabbits away from the vegetable garden, sprinkle scented talcum powder around perimeter and plants.

Ruby Miller, Auburn, KY

Easy Fly Trap

Fill a plastic jar three-quarters full with water. Add ¼ cup apple cider vinegar, 2 tablespoons sugar, and 2 tablespoons dish soap. Place the ends of a very strong string down in the jar, leaving it long enough to hang. Screw on the lid over the string. Punch a few holes in the lid so flies can get in. Hang jar on porch or other places around the yard. Works amazingly well.

Esther Miller, Rossiter, PA

Autumn

Apples • Brussels Sprouts • Cabbage
Carrots • Collards • Cranberries • Grapes
Kale • Kiwi • Pears • Peppers
Pumpkin • Sweet Potatoes

Autumn Recipes

Oh! The feeling of security
That comes to yourself
When you go to your basement
And see a well-filled canning shelf.
LYDIA HERSHBERGER, DALTON, OH

Pumpkin Spice Dip

12 ounces cream
  cheese, softened

4 tablespoons butter,
  softened

¾ cup powdered sugar

1 cup pumpkin puree

1 teaspoon cinnamon

½ teaspoon pumpkin
  pie spice

In a bowl, mix all together and beat until smooth and creamy. Chill 4 hours before serving. Serve with pretzels, chocolate chip cookies, and apple wedges.

KATHRYN TROYER, Rutherford, TN

Pumpkin Latte

1 cup milk
½ cup strong coffee
¼ teaspoon cinnamon or
   pumpkin pie spice
½ teaspoon vanilla

2 tablespoons
   pumpkin puree
1 tablespoon maple syrup
5 drops liquid stevia

Put all ingredients in a saucepan and heat just to boiling. Serve in your favorite mug and enjoy.

Leah Hochstetler, Dundee, OH

Pumpkin Cheesecake Shake

1 cup crushed ice
⅓ cup milk
¼ cup cottage cheese
1 to 2 ounces cream cheese
   or 2 tablespoons heavy
   whipping cream
2 tablespoons
   pumpkin puree

¼ teaspoon pumpkin
   pie spice
Dash vanilla
Dash salt
⅛ teaspoon xanthan gum
3 smidgens stevia
½ scoop whey protein
   powder (optional)

Put all ingredients in a blender and blend until smooth.

Ranae Yoder, Kalona, IA

Fresh Fruit Salsa

Zest of 1 orange
½ cup orange juice
2 packed tablespoons
   brown sugar

2 tablespoons apple jelly
2 apples, peeled and cored
2 kiwi, peeled and diced
1 cup sliced strawberries

In a bowl, mix orange zest, orange juice, brown sugar, and jelly. Toss in apples, kiwi, and strawberries, coating well. Cover and refrigerate.

Esther M. Peachey, Flemingsburg, KY

Fresh 'n' Cool Cranberry Dip

1 (8 ounce) package
    cream cheese
½ cup sour cream

4 to 5 tablespoons sugar
½ cup cranberry relish

In a bowl, mix all ingredients well. Chill, then serve with butter-flavored crackers.

KATHRYN TROYER, Rutherford, TN

Cranberry-Jalapeño Dip

12 ounces cranberries,
    chopped
¼ cup chopped onion
2 green jalapeño peppers,
    deseeded and chopped

2 tablespoons chopped
    cilantro
⅛ teaspoon salt
¾ cup sugar
8 ounces cream cheese
½ cup sour cream

In a bowl, combine cranberries, onion, peppers, and cilantro. Mix in salt and sugar. Allow to set several minutes; drain. In another bowl, blend cream cheese and sour cream. Spread in bottom of a dish. Top with cranberry mixture. Delicious served with crackers.

"A delicacy!"

HANNAH SCHROCK, Salem, MO

Jalapeño Dip

2 (8 ounce) packages cream
    cheese, softened
1 (16 ounce) carton
    sour cream
½ cup salad dressing

5 jalapeños, deseeded
    and chopped
2 cups shredded
    cheddar cheese
1 teaspoon onion powder

In a bowl, combine all ingredients. Pour into a small, greased casserole dish, and bake at 350 degrees for 20 minutes or until bubbly. Serve with crackers or chips.

"Perfect for a barbecue."

MARY BONTRAGER, Middlebury, IN

Pepper Poppers

Banana or jalapeño peppers
Cream cheese
1 egg
2 tablespoons lemon juice
½ teaspoon melted
  shortening

⅔ cup water
1 cup flour
½ teaspoon salt
Oil for frying

Cut peppers in half lengthwise and remove seeds. Fill cavity with cream cheese. In a bowl, blend egg, lemon juice, shortening, water, flour, and salt to make batter. Dip peppers in batter and deep-fry in hot oil.

Mrs. Benjamin Wickey, Monroe, IN

Morning Glory Muffins

2 cups whole wheat flour
2 teaspoons baking soda
½ teaspoon salt
2 teaspoons cinnamon
3 eggs
⅔ cup honey or
   sweetener of choice
½ cup olive oil

½ cup buttermilk
   or sour milk
2 cups finely shredded
   carrots
½ cup raisins (optional)
½ cup shredded coconut
½ cup chopped nuts or
   sunflower seeds
1 apple, grated

In a mixing bowl, combine flour, baking soda, salt, and cinnamon. Add eggs, honey, oil, and buttermilk, stirring until moistened. Fold in carrots, raisins, coconut, nuts, and apple. Spoon into lined muffin tins and bake at 350 degrees for 20 minutes.

MARY ELLEN WENGERD, Campbellsville, KY

Sweet Potato Muffins

1 egg
½ cup milk
½ cup mashed cooked sweet
   potato or pumpkin
¼ cup butter, melted
1½ cups flour

½ cup sugar
2 teaspoons baking powder
½ teaspoon cinnamon
½ teaspoon nutmeg
½ teaspoon salt

In a mixing bowl, beat together egg, milk, sweet potato, and butter. In a separate bowl, combine flour, sugar, baking powder, cinnamon, nutmeg, and salt. Add to first mixture and stir until just moistened. Bake in muffin tins at 350 degrees for 20 minutes. Makes 12 muffins.

ANNA M. BYLER, Commodore, PA

Stay-Soft Apple Butter Spice Cinnamon Rolls

Dough:

2 tablespoons yeast
2½ cups water
⅔ cup oil
⅔ cup sugar
2 teaspoons salt

3 eggs
⅓ cup instant vanilla
   pudding mix
11 cups bread flour, divided

In a large bowl, dissolve yeast in barely warm water. Add oil, sugar, salt, eggs, pudding mix, and 6 cups of flour. Mix with mixer for 5 minutes. Scrape down sides of bowl partway through. Slowly add more flour 1 cup at a time until dough is soft though still sticky. Oil dough and hands well, remove dough from bowl, and let rise in well-oiled mixing bowl until at least doubled. Roll into a large rectangle and spread with filling.

Filling:

1 (8 ounce) package cream
   cheese, softened
½ cup apple butter

2 tablespoons flour
¾ cup brown sugar
1 tablespoon cinnamon

In a bowl, mix cream cheese, apple butter, and flour until smooth. Spread on dough. Sprinkle with brown sugar and cinnamon. Roll up and cut into slices and arrange in greased pans. Let rise until light, fluffy, and more than doubled in size. Bake at 350 degrees for 20 minutes or until golden brown.

Glaze:

2 tablespoons butter,
   browned
1½ cups powdered sugar

1 teaspoon clear vanilla
¼ teaspoon cinnamon
Milk

Mix butter, powdered sugar, vanilla, and cinnamon. Add milk to make it drizzling consistency. Mix well. Pour into plastic zipper bag. Cut off a small corner and drizzle over cooled rolls.

Kathryn Troyer, Rutherford, TN

Overnight Pumpkin French Toast Casserole

½ loaf of 1- to 2-day-old
  bread, cut into 1-inch cubes
6 eggs
1 cup milk
3 tablespoons maple syrup
½ teaspoon vanilla
¼ cup pumpkin puree

1 teaspoon cinnamon
½ teaspoon nutmeg
¼ teaspoon ginger
⅛ teaspoon ground cloves
¼ teaspoon salt
Maple syrup
Powdered sugar

On a cookie sheet, place bread in a single layer and bake at 250 degrees for 15 to 20 minutes until toasted and hardened. Meanwhile, in a blender, blend eggs, milk, maple syrup, vanilla, pumpkin, cinnamon, nutmeg, ginger, cloves, and salt. Place toasted bread in an 8x8-inch baking dish. Pour egg mixture over top and toss with spatula to coat bread. Cover with plastic wrap and refrigerate overnight. In the morning, bake at 350 degrees for 20 to 30 minutes until top is golden brown. Serve warm with maple syrup and powdered sugar.

Anita Lorraine Petersheim, Fredericktown, OH

Apple Salad

8 apples, peeled and diced
2 bananas, chopped
½ cup chopped celery
½ cup raisins
¼ cup shredded coconut
½ cup peanuts
½ cup chopped walnuts

Place all in a bowl and add dressing. Mix well to coat. Serve immediately.

Dressing:

1 cup water
1 teaspoon lemon juice
¼ teaspoon salt
½ cup sugar
1 tablespoon cornstarch
¼ cup heavy cream
1 teaspoon vanilla

In a saucepan, combine ingredients and cook until thickened. Cool.

Anna M. Byler, Commodore, PA

Carrot Salad

3 cups grated carrots
Celery, finely diced
Onion, finely diced
3 hard-boiled eggs, diced
½ cup mayonnaise
1 teaspoon salt
½ cup sugar
¼ tablespoon plain gelatin (to set in a mold, use ½ tablespoon)
½ cup water

In a bowl, mix carrots, celery, onion, eggs, mayonnaise, salt, and sugar. In a saucepan, dissolve gelatin in water and heat, stirring until dissolved. Mix in with carrots. Put in a serving dish and refrigerate several hours.

Feenie Beiler, Delta, PA

Carrot Gelatin Salad

3 small boxes orange gelatin
2 cups boiling water
2½ cups cold water

20 ounces crushed
  pineapple, drained
3 cups finely shredded
  carrots
Cottage cheese

In a bowl, dissolve gelatin in boiling water, then add cold water. Stir well; add pineapple and carrots. Put in a serving bowl and refrigerate overnight. Serve with cottage cheese.

Mary Bontrager, Middlebury, IN

Fruited Coleslaw

1 cup chopped
  unpeeled apple
3 cups shredded cabbage
½ cup drained crushed
  pineapple
¼ cup raisins
½ cup salad dressing

¼ cup pineapple juice
¾ teaspoon celery seed
2 teaspoons sugar
¾ teaspoon mustard
Pinch salt

In a large bowl, mix apple, cabbage, pineapple, and raisins. In a small bowl, combine salad dressing, pineapple juice, celery seed, sugar, mustard, and salt. Pour over cabbage mixture and stir to coat.

Anita Lorraine Petersheim, Fredericktown, OH

Old-Fashioned Coleslaw

3 tablespoons sugar
2 tablespoons flour
1 teaspoon ground mustard
½ teaspoon salt
⅛ teaspoon cayenne pepper
1 egg
¾ cup water
¼ cup lemon juice

1 tablespoon margarine
  or butter
¼ cup sour cream
6 cups shredded cabbage
1 cup shredded carrot
½ cup finely chopped
  bell pepper

In a heavy 1-quart saucepan, mix sugar, flour, mustard, salt, and cayenne. Beat in egg. Gradually stir in water and lemon juice until well blended. Cook over low heat 13 to 15 minutes, stirring constantly, until thick and smooth. Remove from heat. Stir in margarine until melted. Place plastic wrap directly on surface of mixture and refrigerate for 2 hours or until fully cooled. Remove wrap and stir in sour cream. In a large bowl, combine cabbage, carrot, and bell pepper. Pour on dressing and toss to coat well. Refrigerate at least 1 hour but not longer than 24 hours before serving.

Mrs. Lizzie Schwartz, Geneva, IN

IVAN'S SALAD

½ head cabbage, shredded
Tomatoes, chopped
Bacon, fried and crumbled

½ cup finely chopped onion
Cheddar cheese, shredded
Corn chips, crushed

Layer cabbage in a 9x13-inch pan. Spread with dressing. Layer with tomatoes, bacon, onion, and cheese. Just before serving, top with corn chips.

DRESSING:

1 cup salad dressing
¼ teaspoon salt
1½ teaspoons mustard

¼ cup sugar
5 tablespoons milk

Blend all ingredients well.

IVAN YODER, Junction City, OH

LAYERED TACO SALAD

1 (16 ounce) carton
   sour cream
1 (8 ounce) package
   cream cheese
½ package taco seasoning
¾ teaspoon onion powder
¼ teaspoon basil
1 teaspoon parsley flakes

1 cup salsa
Onion, chopped
Green bell pepper, chopped
Tomato, diced
Shredded cheese
Tortilla chips

In a bowl, mix sour cream, cream cheese, taco seasoning, onion powder, basil, and parsley until smooth. Put in a deep-dish pie plate. Spread salsa over top. Sprinkle onion, bell pepper, and tomato on top in amount you desire. Cover with cheese. Garnish with more of the onion, green pepper, and/or tomatoes if desired. Serve with tortilla chips.

"I like to serve this at our Christmas gatherings. This is best if it's prepared a few hours in advance and refrigerated, allowing the flavors to blend."

MARY ANN YUTZY, Bloomfield, IA

CRANBERRY RELISH

1 package frozen cranberries
3 cups sugar
6 to 8 apples

1 (3 ounce) box cherry gelatin
¼ cup orange juice
  concentrate

Grind frozen cranberries. Add sugar. Set aside. Grind apples. Mix into cranberries. Make gelatin according to package directions, replacing some of the water with orange juice concentrate. Chill gelatin until it starts to gel. Add to cranberry mixture. Chill.

ANNA M. BYLER, Commodore, PA

DRESSING (STUFFING)

1 pound loaf bread, cubed
  and lightly toasted
1 cup chopped celery
1 cup chopped carrots
1 cup cooked and
  diced potatoes
1 medium onion, chopped
Celery leaves (optional)

1 quart chicken broth
3 eggs
1 cup milk
½ stick butter or
  margarine, browned
Salt and pepper to taste
Seasoning salt to taste

In a large bowl, combine bread, celery, carrots, potatoes, onions, and celery leaves. In another bowl, mix chicken broth, eggs, milk, and butter. Pour over bread mixture and stir in to moisten all. Season to taste with salt, pepper, and seasoning salt. If bread is too hard and dry, you may need to add more liquid. You can use additional broth, milk, or hot water. Place in a 9x13-inch pan. Bake at 350 degrees for 1 hour.

REBECCA GIROD, Berne, IN

SCALLOPED AUTUMN BAKE

4 cups sweet potatoes,
  cut into ¼-inch slices
2 cups thinly sliced apples
1 cup brown sugar, divided

6 tablespoons butter, divided
½ teaspoon salt, divided
1½ cups small
  marshmallows

In a buttered baking dish, layer half of the sweet potatoes. Cover with half the apples. Sprinkle with ½ cup brown sugar. Dot with 3 tablespoons butter. Sprinkle with ¼ teaspoon salt. Repeat all the layers. Bake at 325 degrees for about 1 hour or until tender. Top with marshmallows and return to oven until marshmallows are puffy or slightly browned.

ROSIE E. SCHWARTZ, Berne, IN

SCALLOPED CABBAGE

3 quarts shaved cabbage
1 cup grated Parmesan
  cheese
1 cup cream of celery soup

1 can evaporated milk
½ can water
Breadcrumbs
Butter

Grease a casserole dish. Spread cabbage on bottom of dish. Sprinkle with cheese. Mix soup, milk, and water and pour over all. Top with buttered breadcrumbs. Bake at 400 degrees for 30 minutes until bubbly and brown.

MRS. ELI A. KURTZ, Dayton, PA

Candied Sweet Potatoes

4 medium sweet potatoes
½ cup sugar
½ cup brown sugar

½ cup butter
½ cup water

Cut sweet potatoes and place in a shallow, greased dish. Combine sugar, brown sugar, butter, and water. Pour over potatoes. Bake at 400 degrees for 20 minutes, stirring several times, until tender.

LEAH YODER, Glenville, PA

Maple Sweet Potatoes

6 sweet potatoes, boiled
1 cup maple syrup

2 tablespoons butter

Pare sweet potatoes and slice. Arrange in a shallow baking pan. Cover with maple syrup and dot with butter. Bake at 450 degrees for 45 minutes.

ANNA BYLER, Spartansburg, PA

Honey-Glazed Sweet Potatoes

2 pounds yams
6 tablespoons butter, melted
1 teaspoon fresh lemon juice

3 tablespoons honey
Salt and pepper to taste

Cut yams into ½- to ¾-inch cubes. In a bowl, mix together butter, lemon juice, honey, and salt and pepper. Pour over yams and mix well. Put in a greased baking dish. Cover and bake at 425 degrees for 20 to 30 minutes, or until yams are soft and tender.

MARY BONTRAGER, Middlebury, IN

Pecan Sweet Potato Bake

3 cups mashed sweet
   potatoes
2 eggs
½ cup sugar

¼ cup half and half
¼ cup butter, softened
2 teaspoons vanilla
⅛ teaspoon salt

In a large mixing bowl, combine all ingredients. Beat until light and fluffy. Transfer to a greased 11x7x2-inch baking dish.

Topping:

½ cup brown sugar
2 tablespoons flour

¼ cup cold butter
½ cup chopped pecans

In a bowl, combine the brown sugar and flour. Cut in butter until crumbly. Fold in pecans and sprinkle on sweet potato mixture. Bake uncovered at 350 degrees for 30 to 35 minutes.

Mary Miller, North Bloomfield, OH

Skillet Sweet Potatoes

4 sweet potatoes
1 cup water
3 tablespoons coconut
   or olive oil
2 teaspoons sea salt

2 teaspoons dried parsley
2 teaspoons pepper
1 teaspoon paprika
1 teaspoon garlic powder

Peel sweet potatoes, if desired. Dice into ½-inch cubes. Heat a skillet over low to medium heat. Add sweet potatoes, water, and oil to skillet. Stir and add salt, parsley, pepper, paprika, and garlic powder. Cover and cook about 12 minutes, stirring occasionally. Remove cover and cook 8 minutes. Keep an eye on it so potatoes don't burn. Stir occasionally so all sides get crispy.

Leah Renae Miller, Millersburg, OH

YAM CASSEROLE

6 medium yams, cut into
  ½- to ¾-inch cubes

1 teaspoon salt

½ cup brown sugar
  (more if needed)

2 teaspoons cinnamon

6 tablespoons butter

Put yams in a steamer until soft. Once soft, whip until fluffy and beat in salt, brown sugar, cinnamon, and butter. When it's fluffy and mixed well, put into a greased baking dish. Bake at 350 degrees for 15 minutes.

"Very good with grilled steak or chicken."

MARY BONTRAGER, Middlebury, IN

STUFFED PEPPERS

1 pound ground beef
¼ cup chopped onion
1½ cups whole kernel corn
1 (8 ounce) can tomato sauce
1 cup rice, cooked
¼ cup steak sauce
Pepper to taste
6 large green bell peppers

Brown meat in skillet and pour off fat. Stir in onion, corn, tomato sauce, rice, steak sauce, and pepper. Set aside. Cut off tops of bell peppers and remove seeds. Spoon meat mixture into peppers and arrange in baking pan. Bake at 350 degrees for 30 to 35 minutes. Makes 6 servings.

IDA B. MILLER, Smicksburg, PA

STUFFED PEPPER CASSEROLE

2 pounds hamburger, browned
1½ cups chopped cabbage
1 large tomato, peeled and chopped
2 large yellow tomatoes, peeled and chopped
1¼ cups uncooked minute rice
1 medium onion, chopped
4 bell peppers, red and green, chopped
2½ cups water
1 tablespoon salt
1 teaspoon pepper
1 cup shredded cheddar cheese

Combine all ingredients except cheese. Pour into baking dish with lid. Top with shredded cheese. Bake at 375 degrees, covered, for 1½ hours or until rice is tender.

LUCY ZIMMERMAN, Orrstown, PA

Dinner in a Pumpkin

1 medium pumpkin
2 tablespoons oil
1 onion, chopped
1 pound bulk sausage
1 pound ground beef
2 tablespoons brown
  sugar (optional)

1 (10 ounce) can cream
  of mushroom soup
2 tablespoons soy sauce
1 (4 ounce) can sliced
  mushrooms, drained
1 cup cooked rice
Salt and pepper to taste

Cut off top of pumpkin; set aside. Clean out seeds and pulp. Scrape clean. Brush a little oil on inside. Sprinkle with salt. In a skillet, heat oil and sauté onion until tender. Add sausage and beef and brown. Simmer 10 minutes then add brown sugar (if using), mushroom soup, soy sauce, mushrooms, and rice. Season with salt and pepper to taste. Spoon into pumpkin and replace top. Bake on a cookie sheet at 325 degrees for 1½ to 2 hours until inside of pumpkin is tender. Place on a platter. Be sure to scrape out pumpkin with filling when serving.

ANITA LORRAINE PETERSHEIM, Fredericktown, OH

Storing Pumpkins and Winter Squash

Lay pumpkins and squash in storage on the same side on which they grew in the garden. The seeds have settled to that side. When the vegetables are placed on the reverse side, the seeds tear away from the sides, causing decay. They say this was practiced by the pioneers.

CRYSTAL ROPP, Kalona, IA

Fresh Apple Bars

3 eggs	½ teaspoon salt
1 cup oil	2 cups chopped fresh apples
1¾ cups sugar	1 cup powdered sugar
2 cups flour	1 teaspoon vanilla
1 teaspoon baking soda	3 tablespoons water
½ teaspoon cinnamon	

In a mixing bowl, blend eggs, oil, and sugar. Beat well. Add flour, baking soda, cinnamon, and salt. Fold in apples. Pour batter into a greased jelly roll pan. Bake at 350 degrees for 25 to 30 minutes. Mix powdered sugar, vanilla, and water and glaze bars while still warm.

JOANN MILLER, Mount Vernon, OH

Tried-and-True Apple Casserole

8 to 10 apples, peeled,
 cored, and halved
½ cup sugar
1 tablespoon flour
½ teaspoon cinnamon

2 tablespoons butter, diced
Raisins (optional)
Walnuts (optional)
½ cup water

Place apples in a greased 2-quart casserole. Set aside. In a bowl, mix sugar, flour, and cinnamon. Sprinkle over apples. Dot with butter. Sprinkle with raisins and walnuts (if desired). Pour water over all. Cover and bake at 350 degrees for 45 to 60 minutes.

Esther M. Peachey, Flemingsburg, KY

Apple Crunch

4 cups chopped apples
4 tablespoons brown sugar
3 tablespoons flour
½ teaspoon cinnamon
1 egg

1 cup flour
¾ cup brown sugar
1 teaspoon baking powder
¼ teaspoon salt
¼ cup butter, melted

Mix apples, 4 tablespoons brown sugar, 3 tablespoons flour, and cinnamon. Put in 8x8-inch pan. In a bowl, beat egg. Add 1 cup flour, ¾ cup brown sugar, baking powder, and salt. Mix until crumbly. Sprinkle over apples. Drizzle butter over top. Bake at 375 degrees for 45 minutes.

Mrs. Lizzie Schwartz, Geneva, IN

Apple Crisp Pie

1 quart apple pie filling
1 (9 inch) unbaked pie shell
¾ cup quick oats
2 tablespoons flour

¼ cup butter
½ teaspoon baking soda
⅔ cup brown sugar

Spoon apple pie filling into unbaked shell. In a bowl, mix oats, flour, butter, baking soda, and brown sugar until crumbly. Put on top of apples. Bake at 350 degrees for 30 minutes until golden. Serve warm with ice cream.

Mary Bontrager, Middlebury, IN

Apple Dapple Cake

1 cup vegetable oil
2 eggs
2 cups sugar
3 cups flour
½ teaspoon salt

1 teaspoon baking soda
3 cups chopped apples
2 teaspoons vanilla
Nuts (optional)

In a bowl, mix oil, eggs, and sugar. Mix in flour, salt, and baking soda. Stir in apples and vanilla. Pour into a greased 9x13-inch pan. Top with nuts (if desired). Bake at 350 degrees for 45 minutes.

Icing:

1 cup brown sugar
¼ cup milk

¼ cup butter or margarine

In a saucepan, cook brown sugar, milk, and butter over medium heat for 2½ minutes. Spread on cake while cake is still slightly warm.

Barbara A. Schwartz, Geneva, IN

Paper Bag Apple Pie

6 cups coarsely sliced
  or chopped apples
½ cup sugar
½ teaspoon nutmeg
2 tablespoons flour

2 tablespoons lemon juice
1 (9 inch) unbaked pie shell
½ cup butter
½ cup brown sugar
½ cup flour

In a bowl, mix apples, sugar, nutmeg, 2 tablespoons flour, and lemon juice. Pour into unbaked pie shell. In a bowl, cut butter into brown sugar and ½ cup flour until crumbs are the size of peas. Sprinkle evenly over apples and pat down around edges. Slide pie into a brown paper grocery bag (or you can use parchment paper) and fold open end under pie or staple closed. The paper should not touch the top or sides of the pie. Set on a cookie sheet. Bake at 425 degrees for 50 minutes.

This bag method keeps the crust from scorching, helps apples bake evenly, and keeps juices from boiling over onto oven and making a mess.

Lena Yoder, McClure, PA

Special Apple Pie

8 medium apples, sliced
1⅔ cups sour cream
1 cup sugar
⅓ cup flour

¼ teaspoon salt
2 teaspoons vanilla
1 egg, beaten
2 (9 inch) unbaked pie shells

In a large bowl, mix apples, sour cream, sugar, flour, salt, vanilla, and egg. Pour into both pie shells. Bake at 450 degrees for 10 minutes. Reduce heat to 350 degrees and bake 30 minutes. Place crumbs on top and bake 15 minutes until lightly browned.

Crumb Topping:

½ cup chopped walnuts
½ cup flour
⅓ cup sugar
⅓ cup brown sugar

1 teaspoon cinnamon
Pinch salt
½ cup butter

In a small bowl, mix together walnuts, flour, sugar, brown sugar, cinnamon, and salt. Cut in butter until crumbly.

Dorcas Marie Yoder, Meyersdale, PA

Virginia Apple Pudding

½ cup butter
¾ cup sugar
1 cup sifted flour
2 teaspoons baking powder
¼ teaspoon salt

¼ teaspoon cinnamon
1 cup milk
2 cups cooked or canned
   apple slices

Melt butter in 2-quart casserole. In a bowl, combine sugar, flour, baking powder, salt, cinnamon, and milk. Pour into casserole dish. Drain apples. Pile toward the center of the dish on the batter. Bake at 375 degrees for 30 to 40 minutes until batter covers apples and crust browns. Serve with milk or whipped cream.

Mary Joyce Petersheim, Fredericktown, OH

Apple Torte

Crust:
½ cup butter, softened
½ cup sugar

1 cup flour
¼ teaspoon vanilla

In a small bowl, mix ingredients and press into an 8x8-inch pan.

Filling:
1 (8 ounce) package cream
   cheese, softened
¼ cup sugar

1 egg, slightly beaten
½ teaspoon vanilla

In a bowl, beat cream cheese, sugar, egg, and vanilla. Pour over crust.

Topping:
½ teaspoon cinnamon
⅓ cup sugar

¼ teaspoon vanilla
4 cups sliced apples

In a bowl, mix cinnamon, sugar, and vanilla. Toss in apples. Layer over cream cheese mixture. Bake at 400 degrees for 25 minutes. Raise heat to 450 degrees for 10 minutes.

Dorcas Marie Yoder, Meyersdale, PA

FALSE MINCE PIE

2 cups raisins	¾ cup vinegar
4 cups water	2 teaspoons cinnamon
4 eggs	¾ teaspoon ground cloves
2 cups corn syrup	1½ teaspoons allspice
2½ cups sugar, divided	1½ teaspoons nutmeg
2 cups chopped apples	4 cups breadcrumbs
½ cup butter	4 (9 inch) unbaked pie shells

In a 4-quart kettle, cook raisins in water until softened. Remove from heat. In a bowl, beat eggs then add corn syrup and 2 cups sugar. Stir into raisins. Add apples, butter, and vinegar. In a bowl, mix remaining ½ cup sugar with cinnamon, cloves, allspice, and nutmeg. Add to raisin mixture. Stir in breadcrumbs. More breadcrumbs can be added to thicken the mixture. Divide into 4 pie shells. Bake at 425 degrees for 15 minutes. Reduce heat to 350 degrees and bake 30 minutes.

KARI DANETTE PETERSHEIM, Fredericktown, OH

PUMPKIN BARS

1 cup oil
2 cups pumpkin puree
2 cups sugar
4 eggs, beaten
2 cups flour

½ teaspoon salt
2 teaspoons cinnamon
2 teaspoons baking powder
1 heaping teaspoon
   baking soda

In a mixing bowl, blend oil, pumpkin, and sugar. Add eggs. Mix in flour, salt, cinnamon, baking powder, and baking soda. Bake at 350 degrees for 20 to 25 minutes. Cool and frost.

FROSTING:

3 ounces cream
   cheese, softened
6 tablespoons butter,
   softened
1 tablespoon heavy cream

1 teaspoon vanilla
2 cups powdered sugar
½ cup chopped pecans

In a bowl, blend cream cheese, butter, heavy cream, and vanilla. Gradually add powdered sugar and pecans, which may also be sprinkled on top.

KATIE YODER, Goshen, IN

PUMPKIN COOKIES

2 cups sugar
1 cup vegetable oil
1½ cups pumpkin puree
2 eggs
1 teaspoon vanilla
3 cups flour

1 teaspoon salt
1 teaspoon baking powder
1 teaspoon baking soda
1½ tablespoons cinnamon
½ tablespoon ginger
½ tablespoon ground cloves

In a mixing bowl, combine sugar and oil. Add pumpkin, eggs, and vanilla. In another bowl, combine flour, salt, baking powder, baking soda, cinnamon, ginger, and cloves. Mix into wet mixture. Drop by tablespoonful onto greased cookie sheet. Bake at 350 degrees for 10 to 12 minutes. Do not overbake.

CARAMEL ICING:

½ cup butter
1 cup brown sugar
¼ cup milk or
   evaporated milk

Pinch salt
1¾ to 2 cups powdered sugar

In a saucepan, melt butter. Add brown sugar and boil over low heat for 2 minutes, stirring constantly. Add milk and salt. Stir until it comes to a complete boil. Remove from heat and cool to lukewarm. Gradually beat in powdered sugar until thick enough to spread. Spread on cooled cookies.

FREDA FISHER, Leola, PA

PUMPKIN PECAN PIE

3 eggs, slightly beaten
1 cup mashed pumpkin
   or winter squash
1 cup sugar
½ cup dark corn syrup

1 teaspoon vanilla
½ teaspoon cinnamon
¼ teaspoon salt
1 (9 inch) unbaked pie shell
1 cup chopped pecans

In a bowl, combine eggs, pumpkin, sugar, corn syrup, vanilla, cinnamon, and salt. Mix well. Pour into pie shell. Top with pecans. Bake at 350 degrees for about 40 minutes or until a knife inserted halfway between center and edge comes out clean.

DORCAS MARIE YODER, Meyersdale, PA

PUMPKIN PIE CAKE

1 box yellow cake mix
½ cup butter, melted
1 egg, beaten
3 cups pumpkin puree
3 eggs
¼ cup sugar

½ cup brown sugar
⅔ cup milk
1½ teaspoons cinnamon
½ cup butter
½ cup chopped nuts

Reserve 1 cup cake mix for topping; set aside. In a bowl, mix remaining cake mix with ½ cup butter and 1 egg. Press into a 9x13-inch pan. In another bowl, mix pumpkin, 3 eggs, sugar, brown sugar, milk, and cinnamon. Beat well. Spread over bottom layer. To reserved 1 cup of cake mix, add ½ cup butter and nuts. Mix until crumbs form, and spread on top of pumpkin layer. Bake at 350 degrees for 50 to 55 minutes.

ANNA M. BYLER, Commodore, PA

PUMPKIN CRUNCH

1 (15 ounce) can pumpkin
1 (12 ounce) can
   evaporated milk
1 teaspoon cinnamon
1 cup sugar

3 eggs, beaten
1 package yellow cake mix
1 cup chopped pecans
1 cup (2 sticks) butter,
   cut into pieces

In a large mixing bowl, whisk together pumpkin, evaporated milk, cinnamon, and sugar until well combined. Add eggs and mix well. Pour mixture into a greased 9x13-inch pan. Sprinkle cake mix evenly over the entire top. Sprinkle evenly with nuts and top with butter. Bake at 350 degrees for 50 to 60 minutes. Cool.

FROSTING:

1 (8 ounce) package cream
   cheese, softened
1 cup heavy cream

½ cup powdered sugar
½ teaspoon cinnamon

In a large mixing bowl, whip cream cheese until light. Add cream and continue to whip until fully combined and thickening. Add powdered sugar and cinnamon. Whip until smooth. Frost the cooled cake.

REBECCA GIROD, Berne, IN

Pumpkin Custard Pie

1 tablespoon flour
½ cup sugar
½ cup brown sugar
¼ teaspoon salt
½ teaspoon cinnamon

1 cup pumpkin puree
2 eggs, separated
2 cups heavy cream
1 unbaked pie shell

In a bowl, mix flour, sugar, brown sugar, salt, and cinnamon. Stir in pumpkin and egg yolks. Add cream. Mix well. In another bowl, beat egg whites to peaks. Fold into pumpkin puree. Pour into unbaked pie shell. Bake at 425 degrees for 10 minutes. Reduce heat to 350 degrees and bake for 20 minutes longer, or until middle is just a little shaky.

RACHEL SCHLABACH, Millersburg, OH

Pumpkin Torte

BASE:

2 packs graham crackers,
  crumbled finely
⅓ cup brown sugar
½ cup margarine, melted

2 eggs
¾ cup sugar
1 (8 ounce) package cream
  cheese, softened

In a bowl, combine graham cracker crumbs, brown sugar, and margarine. Pat into 9x13-inch pan. In another bowl, beat eggs. Add sugar and cream cheese, beating until smooth. Pour on top of crumbs. Bake at 300 degrees for 20 minutes. Cool.

FILLING:

1 package unflavored gelatin
¼ cup water
2 cups pumpkin puree
3 egg yolks, well beaten
⅔ cup sugar
½ cup milk

½ teaspoon salt
1 teaspoon cinnamon
3 egg whites
¼ cup sugar
Whipped topping

In a bowl, dissolve gelatin in water; set aside. In saucepan, beat together pumpkin, egg yolks, ⅔ cup sugar, milk, salt, and cinnamon. Bring to a boil until thickened. Remove from heat. Add dissolved gelatin. Cool. In a bowl, beat egg whites with ¼ cup sugar. Fold into cooled pumpkin mixture. Spread over cooled cream cheese base. Top with whipped cream.

NORMA YUTZY, Drakesville, IA

Pumpkin Bread Trifle with Pomegranate Seeds

3¾ cups sugar, divided
2 cups pumpkin puree
1 cup vegetable oil
4 eggs
⅔ cup water
3⅓ cups flour
2 teaspoons baking soda
2 teaspoons pumpkin
  pie spice
1 teaspoon salt
1½ cups chopped pecans
2 tablespoons water
2½ cups heavy cream
1 (8 ounce) carton sour cream
1 cup powdered sugar
2 tablespoons milk
1 loaf bread
Pomegranate seeds
Caramel ice cream topping

In a large bowl, stir together 3 cups sugar, pumpkin, oil, eggs, and water. In a medium bowl, whisk together flour, baking soda, pumpkin pie spice, and salt. Stir into pumpkin mixture. Spoon into 3 greased 5x9-inch loaf pans. Bake at 325 degrees for 45 to 60 minutes. Let cool for 10 minutes. Remove from pans.

Grease a baking sheet and scatter pecans on it close together. In a saucepan, combine 2 tablespoons water and remaining ¾ cup sugar; cook 6 minutes without stirring but brushing sides of pan with water. Pour over pecans. Cool and break apart.

In a bowl, combine heavy cream, sour cream, powdered sugar, and milk. Beat to blend; continue until peaks form.

Cut bread into cubes. In a trifle bowl, layer bread cubes, pudding mixture, pecans, pomegranate seeds, and caramel sauce.

You can also layer in fancy little glass cups for individual servings.

"Something special and different for the holidays."

Lorene Byler, Irvington, KY

Sweet Potato Pie

3 tablespoons flour
1⅔ cups sugar
1 cup smashed cooked
   sweet potato
2 eggs
¼ cup light corn syrup

¼ teaspoon nutmeg
Pinch salt
½ cup butter
¾ cup evaporated milk
1 (9 inch) unbaked pie shell

In a large mixing bowl, combine flour and sugar. Add sweet potato, eggs, corn syrup, nutmeg, salt, butter, and milk. Beat well. Pour into pie shell. Bake at 350 degrees for 50 to 60 minutes until a knife inserted in the middle comes out clean.

Dorcas Marie Yoder, Meyersdale, PA

SAUERKRAUT

5 pounds cabbage   3½ tablespoons salt

Shred cabbage with shredder or sharp knife. The cabbage should be no thicker than a dime. Sprinkle salt over the cabbage and mix thoroughly by hand. Pack into clean glass jars, pressing the cabbage down firmly with a wooden spoon. Be sure the juice covers the cabbage. Wipe off the jars and put on lids. Don't seal tightly. Set the filled jars in shallow pans to catch the brine that may overflow during fermentation. Set in the basement for 1 week or until liquid settles and bubbles no longer rise to the surface. Remove lids and clean the jar tops and lids. Adjust the lids to tighten. Process in boiling water bath for 10 minutes to seal.

JUDY ZIMMERMAN, East Earl, PA

CANNING POTATOES

Peel and shred potatoes. Wash potatoes in 3 different baths of cold water to remove as much starch as possible. Then put through a salad spinner to remove all water. Fill sterile jars with potatoes. To 1 quart potatoes add 1 teaspoon salt and 1 tablespoon white vinegar. Seal jars by cold-packing in boiling water for 15 minutes. These are sure to keep, and they taste better than those without the vinegar that are cold-packed for 2 hours.

LINDA BURKHOLDER, Fresno, OH

CREAM OF MUSHROOM SOUP

2 cups butter
8 cups chopped mushrooms
1 large onion, chopped
6 cloves garlic, chopped
1 gallon milk

3 teaspoons salt
½ teaspoon pepper
2 cups flour
4 cups water

In a skillet, simmer butter, mushrooms, onion, and garlic until browned. In a saucepan, heat milk. Add mushrooms to milk along with salt and pepper. In a bowl, use eggbeater to mix flour and water. Slowly add to boiling milk and cook until thick.

Pour into 12 sterilized pint jars. Seal with 2-part lids. Seal in pressure canner at 10 pounds for 30 minutes.

MRS. KRISTINA BYLER, Crab Orchard, KY

BAKED APPLE BUTTER

7 pounds apples or 4
  quarts applesauce
2 tablespoons cinnamon
6 cups brown sugar

½ cup vinegar or cider
1 cup crushed
  pineapple, drained

When using fresh apples, cook until soft, cool, and put through sieve. Add cinnamon, sugar, vinegar, and pineapple to applesauce and mix well. Pour into baking dish, cover, and bake at 350 degrees for 3 hours, stirring occasionally. Pour into jars and seal. Note: Recipe may be tripled to make a large batch and will fit into a 13-quart stainless-steel bowl.

MRS. DANIEL GINGERICH, Rensselaer Falls, NY

OVER-100-YEAR-OLD APPLE RELISH

16 cups cored and
  ground apples
8 cups ground onions

2 cups hot red peppers
  (jalapeño or other)
8 cups vinegar
12 cups sugar

Core and grind apples. Grind onions and peppers. Combine all ingredients and cook in large kettle until mixture thickens. Simmer for 45 minutes to 1 hour, stirring constantly. If mixture becomes dry, add a little more vinegar. Skim off foam. Pour into sterilized jars and seal in a hot water bath for 15 minutes.

SHARRI NOBLETT, Port Arthur, TX

Apple Pie Filling

6 cups sugar
5 heaping tablespoons
   instant Clear Jel
2 tablespoons cinnamon
Pinch salt

16 cups peeled and sliced
   or chopped apples
¼ cup lemon juice
1 quart water

Mix sugar and Clear Jel thoroughly. Add cinnamon and salt. Pour over apples. Mix lemon juice and water. Pour over apples. Mix all together. Let stand 10 minutes. Pour into jars and seal in a hot water bath for 10 minutes.

Mrs. Amanda Byler, Curwensville, PA

Grape Butter

4 cups grapes, crushed

4 cups sugar

In a bowl, combine grapes and sugar and let set overnight. Place in saucepan and cook for 20 minutes; put through sieve. Bring mixture back to a boil. Pour into small jars and seal in a hot water bath for 10 minutes.

Mrs. Levi Gingerich, Dalton, OH

Green Tomato Relish

18 green tomatoes, quartered
8 red bell peppers, quartered
4 green bell peppers,
   quartered
6 onions, quartered
3 cups vinegar

3 cups sugar
1 tablespoon celery seed
1 cup water
1½ tablespoons salt
4 tablespoons prepared
   mustard

Grind tomatoes, peppers, and onions; drain well. Add vinegar, sugar, celery seed, water, and salt to ground mixture. Pour into saucepan and cook for 15 minutes. Combine mustard with a little water or milk and add to cooked mixture. Cook 2 minutes longer. Pour into jars and seal in a hot water bath for 15 minutes. Use like ketchup.

Annetta Martin, New Holland, PA

FERMENTED CHOP

1 gallon sweet peppers,
    cut into strips
2 hot peppers (optional)
Other vegetables of choice,
    chopped (cauliflower,
    cucumber, carrot, etc.)
5 cups water

5 cups vinegar
1 cup salt
2 cups olive oil
2½ to 3 tablespoons
    chopped garlic
¼ cup oregano flakes

Place sweet peppers, hot peppers, and other vegetables in a bowl. In separate bowl, mix water, vinegar, salt, olive oil, garlic, and oregano. Pour over vegetables. Let set 24 hours to marinate. It will create more juice in that time. Divide vegetables into jars and fill to the top with brine, leaving as little air space as possible to help preserve in storage. Put on plastic lids. No need to heat or to seal jars. Should keep up to a year. Can be stored on cellar shelves.

ELAM AND SARAH BEILER, Doylesburg, PA

Canned Peppers

28 ounces ketchup
2 cups vinegar
1 or 2 cups sugar
1 clove garlic

1 cup oil
1 tablespoon salt (optional)
1 gallon chopped hot peppers
  or sweet bell peppers

In a stockpot, combine ketchup, vinegar, sugar, garlic, oil, and salt. Bring to a boil. Add peppers and cook for 5 minutes. Do not cook until peppers soften. Pack into canning jars and seal in a hot water bath.

"When we open a jar, we heat the pepper and eat it with salad dressing on bread. Very delicious. Also, sliced or chopped hot dogs can be added to the peppers before canning."

FANNIE ANN HOSTETLER, Brookville, PA

BANANA PEPPERS

Banana peppers
1 quart water
3 quarts vinegar
1 cup brown sugar

1 cup salt
1 cup mustard
½ teaspoon alum

Pack banana peppers whole or cut in jars. In a stockpot, heat water, vinegar, brown sugar, salt, mustard, and alum to boiling. Pour over peppers. Heat can lids to put on. No need to cold-pack.

MARILYN LAMBRIGHT, Goshen, IN

HOT PEPPER BUTTER

40 hot peppers (I replace
   half with sweet peppers)
6 cups sugar
1 quart vinegar

1 quart prepared mustard
1 tablespoon salt
1½ cups flour
1½ cups water

Remove seeds from peppers while wearing protective gloves. Grind peppers and mix in a stockpot with sugar, vinegar, mustard, and salt. Boil 10 to 15 minutes. In a bowl, mix flour and water. Slowly add to boiling mixture. Boil 5 minutes. Stir thoroughly because it will stick to bottom easily. Pour into jars while hot.

"A good sandwich spread. We also enjoy mixing hot pepper butter with cream cheese to eat on crackers."

ELLA ARLENE YODER, Arcola, IL

SUGAR CURE FOR BACON

4 gallons water
2 pounds brown sugar

6 pounds salt
1 ounce saltpeter

In a stockpot, bring water to a boil. Add brown sugar, salt, and saltpeter. Let cool. Put brine in a barrel. Put slabs of raw bacon in the brine and weigh down to keep them covered. Let brine for 4 days then smoke for 1 day.

KATIE MILLER, Apple Creek, OH

BRINE FOR BACON AND HAM

4½ gallons water
3 cups salt
2¼ cups brown sugar

⅜ cup baking soda
¼ cup pepper
¾ cup vinegar

In a stockpot, mix all together until dissolved. In a pail, cover bacon and ham with brine. Place in a cool place for 2 to 3 weeks before smoking meat.

We also use this brine for our Thanksgiving turkey. Make sure brine covers turkey and leave it for 2 to 3 days in a cool place. When you are ready to bake, put bacon slices over the turkey with toothpicks to hold bacon in place. Bake at 250 to 300 degrees until done. Time is based on size of turkey.

HANNAH SCHROCK, Salem, MO

Fall Harvest Décor

On a sunny, fall day, when leaves are turning, visit a local farmers' market to see the great bounty of the autumn harvest. Choose squash, corn, apples, and pumpkins. To create a beautiful scene on your porch or yard, buy some gourds, Indian corn, bittersweets, cornstalks, and pumpkins of all sizes. Mix it all together for great fall arrangements.

Kathryn Detweiler, West Farmington, OH

Baking Tips

Best Baking Soda

To test if baking soda is still good, drop ½ teaspoon baking soda in ½ cup boiling water. If it sizzles, it is good. If not, replace it.

CRYSTAL ROPP, Kalona, IA

Butter Tip

Slicing a stick of butter very thinly will help it soften quickly.

ELLA MILLER, Big Prairie, OH

Fat-Free Baking

Substitute thick applesauce in equal amounts for the shortening or oil called for in a recipe for a fat-free cake or sweet bread.

MRS. EMANUEL SCHMIDT, Carlisle, KY

Hard Cookies

If your cookies get too hard, add some pieces of bread to the airtight cookie container, and the cookies will soften.

ELLA MILLER, Big Prairie, OH

Nonstick Cooking Spray

Mix equal parts liquid lecithin and olive oil. Brush into your cookware and bakeware for nonstick cooking. Very little is needed. Note: Liquid lecithin can be purchased at most health food stores and some bulk food stores.

MIRIAM MILLER, Stanford, KY

All the Seasons Have Special Blessings!

AUTUMN AND WINTER

Here in Indiana, with fall coming upon us, I think of the colorful leaves—oh, such beauty! Also I appreciate the many rewards we've received from our summer work. Lots of canned fruits and veggies fill our basement shelves.

A big part of our Amish heritage is knowing how to preserve food to share with family and friends. As we dig potatoes, sweet potatoes, carrots, and other in-ground vegetables and gather up wagonloads of pumpkins, squash, colorful gourds, and ears of colored corn, we experience our reward for pulling weeds in the summer's warm sun. This is all in preparing to fill our Thanksgiving table for family and friends. Each year, more precious memories are added, along with our thanks, and mentioned to God.

But keep in mind the old saying of "all work and no play" makes "Jack" a sad and weary boy. So, before fall turns cold, take time to make "lasting memories." Fill a basket with fruits, veggies, and juices, and head out for a picnic or go to the lake for a ride. If your picnic takes you to a pond or lake, take a fishing pole to try your luck. Build a fire and relax with s'mores. In case you forgot to buy cookies or graham crackers for s'mores, try using snack crackers and a jar of peanut butter.

Once the leaves fall from the trees with frosty evening air and are raked on a pile and the gardens are empty, start planning for the holidays! Christmas, New Year's, and Epiphany, which is January 6. It is referred to as "Old Christmas" and commemorates the day the wise men arrived with gifts for baby Jesus. Don't get too busy that you forget "family time."

Now sit back and enjoy the winter weather. Let it snow while you bake cookies, sew, and do fun hobbies like puzzles and games, to mention a few. And a plate of goodies taken to a shut-in does wonders to lift a dreary day.

K.Y., Goshen, IN

WINTER

Citrus • Home Canned Goods
Nuts • Onions • Potatoes
Turnips • Winter Squash

WINTER RECIPES

*"Life is like an onion; you peel off one layer
at a time and sometimes you weep."*

RHODA MILLER, DECATUR, IN

CHRISTMAS PUNCH

1 (12 ounce) can frozen
    orange juice concentrate

1 (12 ounce) can frozen
    lemonade concentrate

1 (46 ounce) can
    pineapple juice

4 cups water

4 quarts lemon-
    lime soda pop

Mix orange juice and lemonade concentrates, pineapple juice, and water. Freeze. When ready to serve. Place in a large bowl and cover with soda pop.

MRS. AMANDA BYLER, Curwensville, PA

GINGER ALE

2 gallons water
3 pounds sugar
3 teaspoons ginger

Juice of 4 lemons
⅛ teaspoon yeast

In a stockpot, mix water, sugar, ginger, and lemon juice. Bring to boil for 3 minutes. Cool. Add yeast and stir well. Strain if desired. Pour into pint-sized or smaller bottles and put on caps. Keep in a warm place for 48 hours. Store in cellar or cold place until you are ready to drink.

MRS. REUBEN (MARTHA) BYLER, Atlantic, PA

Cappuccino Mocha Mix

4 cups nondairy coffee
    creamer powder
2½ cups nonfat dry milk
1 cup sugar
¾ cup instant coffee
1 cup chocolate drink powder

½ cup powdered sugar
Dash salt
⅔ cup instant vanilla
    pudding mix
16 ounces french vanilla
    creamer powder

Mix all ingredients together. Stir ⅓ cup mixture into 1 cup hot water for a delicious drink.

Marilyn Lambright, Goshen, IN

Quick Mocha

Make your own Swiss mocha drink by using 1 teaspoon instant coffee and 1 teaspoon hot cocoa mix. It's delicious!

Joanna D. Miller, Loudonville, OH

CHRISTMAS SALAD

2 small boxes
  strawberry gelatin
1 (20 ounce) can crushed
  pineapple
½ cup chopped pecans
1 package unflavored
  gelatin, dissolved in
  ¼ cup cold water

1 (8 ounce) package cream
  cheese, softened
1 cup whipping cream
Dash sugar
Vanilla to taste
2 small boxes lime gelatin

Mix strawberry gelatin with water according to package directions and pour into 9x13-inch cake pan. Let cool in refrigerator to jelly stage. Drain pineapple and save juice. Put half of pineapple and half of nuts in red gelatin and let set. Bring pineapple juice to a boil and add unflavored gelatin that has been dissolved in ¼ cup cold water. Add cream cheese to gelatin and let cool until partially set. Whip whipping cream until stiff. Add sugar and vanilla then add to juice and gelatin mixture. Pour on top of red gelatin. Let set. Fix lime gelatin as you did the red, and when it is thickened, put on top of juice and cream mixture and let set until hard. Cut to serve.

ALICE BEECHY, Pittsford, MI

Frozen Strawberries Tip

Do your strawberries get rubbery after being frozen like mine do? Don't throw them out. Thaw them and squeeze out the juice. Heat the juice and stir in sugar and Perma Flo paste until your desired thickness. Stir in the strawberries until no globs of strawberries remain. Cool and use as fruit filling.

LENA TROYER, Redding, IA

BBQ Green Beans

4 slices bacon
1 small onion, chopped
½ cup ketchup
¼ cup brown sugar

1 tablespoon
  Worcestershire sauce
1 quart canned green
  beans, drained

In a skillet, fry bacon and onion. Add ketchup, brown sugar, and Worcestershire sauce. Simmer for 3 minutes. In a casserole, spread beans evenly and pour sauce on top. Bake at 350 degrees for 20 minutes.

Marilyn Lambright, Goshen, IN

Ultimate Green Beans

2 quarts canned green beans
¼ cup butter
¼ cup milk
½ pound processed cheese
¾ teaspoon Greek seasoning

½ teaspoon pepper
¼ teaspoon seasoned salt
½ cup butter
1¾ cups crushed crackers

Drain green beans. Put beans into a 9x13-inch greased baking dish. In a saucepan, combine ¼ cup butter, milk, processed cheese, Greek seasoning, pepper, and seasoned salt and mix well over medium heat until melted and smooth. Pour over beans. Bake at 350 degrees for 20 to 30 minutes. Once baked, remove from oven. In a skillet, melt ½ cup butter and stir in crackers, toasting them over medium heat. Sprinkle crumbs on green beans when ready to serve. If you serve in serving bowl, put crumbs on after you put it in the bowl to serve.

Mary Bontrager, Middlebury, IN

HASHBROWN PATTIES

3 tablespoons flour
1 tablespoon minced onion
¼ cup heavy cream
1 teaspoon salt

¼ teaspoon pepper
3 cups finely chopped
  cooked potatoes
3 tablespoons shortening

In a bowl, mix flour, onion, cream, salt, and pepper until smooth. Fold in potatoes, stirring to coat. In a skillet, melt shortening over high heat. Use ¼ cup potato mixture to form a patty ¼ inch thick. Repeat with remaining mixture. Fry each patty until nicely browned on both sides.

KARI DANETTE PETERSHEIM, Fredericktown, OH

Grilled Potatoes

½ cup butter
1 teaspoon salt
½ teaspoon pepper
2 teaspoons parsley flakes

½ teaspoon garlic powder
Potatoes, cut into
1-inch cubes

In a bowl, blend butter, salt, pepper, parsley, and garlic powder. Sprinkle over potatoes and toss to coat. Divide serving sizes onto 6 squares of aluminum foil. Fold into packets. Grill for 15 to 30 minutes, depending on temperature, until tender. Yields 6 servings.

Mrs. Amanda Byler, Curwensville, PA

Homemade Mo-Jos

6 medium potatoes
Milk
1 teaspoon paprika
Dash salt

2 teaspoons seasoned salt
1 teaspoon baking powder
1 cup flour
½ cup butter, melted

Wash and cut potatoes in long pieces. Dip in milk. In a bowl, combine paprika, salt, seasoned salt, baking powder, and flour. Place potatoes in a bag and toss with dry mixture until they are coated. Pour half of butter on bottom of cookie sheet. Place potatoes on the sheet and drizzle with remaining butter. Bake at 400 degrees for 45 minutes. Serve with ketchup or ranch dressing.

Mary Ann Yutzy, Bloomfield, IA

Homemade Tater Tots

4 medium potatoes,
   peeled and cut
1 teaspoon salt

¼ cup flour
Cooking oil

In a saucepan, cook potatoes in water until soft. Drain. Add salt and flour. Mash and mix well. Pack mixture in small cookie scoop to make tots. Deep-fry tots in hot oil until golden brown.

Clara Yoder, Sugar Grove, PA

MASHED POTATOES

6 quarts potatoes, cooked
Milk, warmed

1 (8 ounce) package cream
  cheese, softened
1 cup sour cream

Mash potatoes. Add enough milk to make them fairly thin. Add cream cheese and sour cream.

Can be refrigerated up to 2 days before a dinner. Will also freeze well. Put into a roaster pan and heat slowly at a low temperature in the oven.

KATIE MILLER, Arthur, IL

PARSLEY POTATOES

10 medium potatoes, peeled
2 teaspoons garlic powder
2 tablespoons parsley flakes
Salt and pepper to taste
¼ cup butter, melted

½ cup fried and
  crumbled bacon
1 cup shredded
  cheddar cheese

Cut potatoes into chunks and put into a baking dish. Sprinkle with garlic powder and parsley. Salt and pepper to taste. Drizzle with butter and top with bacon crumbles. Cover and bake at 350 degrees for 45 minutes to 1 hour. Remove from oven. Sprinkle with cheese. Cover until cheese is melted.

MARY BONTRAGER, Middlebury, IN

SOUR CREAM DRESSING FOR POTATOES

1 cup mayonnaise
1 cup sour cream
1½ tablespoons onion powder

1½ tablespoons
  parsley flakes
1½ teaspoons dill weed
1½ teaspoons seasoned salt

Mix all together and serve on baked potatoes.

MARY JOYCE PETERSHEIM, Fredericktown, OH

Italian Spaghetti Squash

1 medium spaghetti squash
1 large jar marinara sauce
½ green bell pepper, diced
¼ cup chopped green onions
½ cup grated carrots

½ cup chopped fresh
  mushrooms
¼ cup chopped black olives
Salt and pepper to taste

Cut spaghetti squash in half, remove seeds, and steam or bake until tender. To bake, place on greased cookie sheet cut-side down. Bake at 350 degrees for 45 to 60 minutes until skin can be pierced with a fork. In a saucepan, heat marinara sauce and add bell pepper, onions, carrots, mushrooms, and black olives. Season to taste with salt and pepper. Once the vegetables are cooked tender, use a fork to scrape spaghetti squash out of shell (being sure to discard any seeds) into a large bowl. Pour sauce over individual servings of squash. Yields 4 servings.

Wanda E. Brunstetter

Buttery Onion Soup

2 cups thinly sliced onions
½ cup butter
¼ cup flour
2 cups chicken broth
2 cups milk

1½ cups processed
  cheese, shredded
Salt and pepper to taste
Parsley flakes (optional)

In a large kettle, sauté onions and butter on low heat until tender, about 15 minutes. Blend in flour and add broth and milk. Cook and stir on medium heat until bubbly. Cook and stir for 1 minute. Reduce heat to low; add cheese and stir until melted. Add salt and pepper. Garnish with parsley flakes and serve. Yields 1½ quarts (6 servings).

MIRIAM YODER, Houstonia, MO

CHEESEBURGER SOUP

4 pounds hamburger, fried
1½ cups chopped onions
3 cups chopped celery
3 cups chopped carrots
9 cups chopped potatoes

2 cups chicken broth
4 cups water
3 teaspoons salt
1½ teaspoons pepper

In a 12-quart stockpot, bring hamburger, onions, celery, carrots, potatoes, broth, and water to boil. Add salt and pepper. Meanwhile, make sauce. When vegetables are soft, pour the sauce over and stir all together. If too thick, add more milk or water to reach desired consistency.

WHITE SAUCE:

1 cup butter
1¾ cups flour
6 cups milk
6 cups processed cheese

1 teaspoon onion salt
1 teaspoon Greek seasoning
½ teaspoon garlic salt

In a saucepan, melt butter and add flour. Slowly add milk. Cook until thick. Add cheese and stir until melted. Add onion salt, Greek seasoning, and garlic salt.

This soup can be frozen.

MARY ANN YUTZY, Bloomfield, IA

Hearty Hamburger Soup

2 pounds ground
  beef, browned
2 cups diced carrots
2 cups diced potatoes
1 cup chopped onion
1 cup chopped celery

1 quart tomato juice
2 teaspoons salt
¼ teaspoon pepper
2 or more cups milk
⅔ cup flour

In a large pot, combine beef, carrots, potatoes, onion, celery, tomato juice, salt, and pepper. Cook until vegetables are tender. In a bowl, slowly combine 2 cups milk and flour. Add to soup. Add 2 to 4 cups more milk if needed to reach desired consistency. Remove from heat. Serve hot.

Bethany Martin, Homer City, PA

Hearty Ham Soup

1 cup diced carrots
½ cup chopped celery
½ cup chopped onions
1 cup diced potatoes
¼ cup butter
1½ teaspoons chicken base
1½ cups diced ham

1 quart milk
2 tablespoons cornstarch
  (or 6 tablespoons flour)
1 cup (4 ounces) shredded
  processed cheese,
  more or less to taste

In a saucepan, combine carrots, celery, onions, potatoes, butter, and chicken base. Cover with water. Cook until vegetables are tender. Add ham and milk. Bring to a boil. Combine cornstarch with a bit of water to liquefy. Stir in to thicken soup. Add as much processed cheese as you want and stir to melt.

Ruth Hochstetler, Dundee, OH

Ham and Cheese Sticky Buns

½ cup butter
⅓ cup brown sugar
2 tablespoons poppy seeds
2 tablespoons mustard

1 package hot dog rolls
 (don't separate)
Sliced ham and cheese

To make the sauce: In a saucepan, cook together butter, brown sugar, poppy seeds, and mustard for 2 minutes. Slice rolls through middle crosswise and layer with ham and cheese. Brush top with all the sauce. Bake at 350 degrees, uncovered, for 20 minutes.

Homemade Buns for Ham and Cheese Sticky Buns

2 packages yeast
1 cup warm water
1 cup scalded milk or
  starch water from
  cooking potatoes
⅔ cup sugar

6 cups flour
½ teaspoon salt
2 eggs
½ cup margarine or
  vegetable shortening

In a large bowl, mix yeast in warm water to dissolve. Add milk and sugar, stirring until sugar dissolves. Add flour and salt. Work in eggs and margarine to form a dough. Let rise until double in size. Knead and form into buns. Let rise again. Spray pans before putting buns in. Bake at 350 degrees for 15 to 20 minutes. This recipe is enough dough for about 24 buns or 2 recipes of Ham and Cheese Sticky Buns.

"Sticky buns are delicious with soup on a cold winter's eve."
MARY AND KATIE YODER, Goshen, IN

SCALLOPED POTATOES AND PORK CHOPS

5 cups peeled and thinly
   sliced raw potatoes
1 cup chopped onion
Salt and pepper to taste

1 can cream of
   mushroom soup
½ cup sour cream
6 pork loin chops
   (1 inch thick)

In greased 9x13-inch baking pan, layer half the potatoes and onion and sprinkle with salt and pepper. Repeat layer. Combine soup and sour cream and pour over potatoes. Cover and bake at 375 degrees for 30 minutes. Meanwhile, in skillet, brown pork chops on both sides. Place pork chops on top of casserole. Cover and return to oven for 45 minutes or until pork chops are tender. Uncover during last 15 minutes of baking. Yields 6 servings.

MRS. ENOS CHRISTNER, Bryant, IN

Potato Pancake Pizza

4 cups shredded potatoes
1 egg, lightly beaten
3 tablespoons flour
1½ tablespoons grated onion
1 teaspoon salt
¼ teaspoon pepper

¼ cup bacon grease
Pizza sauce
Chopped onions
Cooked meat of choice
Shredded cheese

Rinse potatoes in cold water and drain well. Add egg, flour, onion, salt, and pepper. In a frying pan, melt bacon grease. Add a layer of potato batter as you would when making pancakes. Fry until golden brown then flip and fry until done. Top with pizza sauce, onions, meat, and cheese. Allow cheese to melt. Serve immediately.

Another option is to use a variety of finely chopped or grated fresh vegetables and salad dressing for topping the potato pancake.

K. Hertzler, West Salisbury, PA

Skillet Squash Dinner

½ stick butter
½ pound hamburger
1 large onion, chopped

1 butternut squash,
    thinly sliced or diced
Salt and pepper to taste
Cheese, shredded

In a skillet, melt butter and add hamburger, onion, and squash. Cover tightly with lid. Stir every 5 minutes until done. More butter may be needed. Add salt and pepper. Sprinkle with cheese and cover skillet until it melts. Serve immediately.

Mary Ann Yutzy, Bloomfield, IA

CHICKEN PATTIES

3 cups shredded
  cooked chicken
½ cup mayonnaise
2 tablespoons lemon juice

½ cup minced onion
½ teaspoon salt
¾ cup cracker crumbs
Oil

Combine chicken, mayonnaise, lemon juice, onion, and salt. Make into 8 patties. Dip into cracker crumbs and fry in an oiled skillet on both sides until golden brown. Good served with coleslaw.

DARLENE STAUFFER, Elkhorn, KY

CHICKEN DUMPLINGS

2 cups chopped mixed
  vegetables (potatoes,
  carrots, celery, and onions)
1 cup chopped raw chicken

Water
Salt and chicken
  flavoring to taste

Cook vegetables until soft. Place chicken in 3-quart saucepan and cover with water; add salt and chicken flavoring. Heat to boiling and cook until chicken is done. Add vegetables and bring back to a boil before adding dumpling dough.

DUMPLINGS:

1½ cups flour
⅓ cup butter, softened
1 teaspoon salt

2 teaspoons baking powder
2 teaspoons sugar
Milk

Combine flour, butter, salt, baking powder, and sugar. Add enough milk to make a stiff dough. Drop by spoonful onto boiling chicken mixture. Cover and reduce heat for 20 minutes without lifting lid.

ADA MILLER, Norwalk, WI

CHICKEN PIE

2 cups chicken broth
2 tablespoons flour
2 cups diced cooked potatoes
2 cups diced cooked carrots
2 cups cooked peas

2 tablespoons chopped
  cooked celery
1 small onion, chopped
  and cooked
2 cups diced cooked chicken
Buttered breadcrumbs
  or pie dough

In a saucepan, heat broth. Add flour to make a thin gravy. Add potatoes, carrots, peas, celery, onion, and chicken. Pour mixture into baking pan and cover with breadcrumbs or pie dough rolled out to fit oblong baking pan. Bake at 350 degrees for 1 hour.

REBEKAH MAST, Amelia, VA

FROZEN LEMON DESSERT

CRUST:

2 cups graham
   cracker crumbs

2 tablespoons sugar
   (optional)
½ cup butter, melted

In a bowl, mix crumbs, sugar (if using), and melted butter. Reserve about ½ cup crumbs and press remaining in bottom of 9-inch square pan.

FILLING:

1¼ cups sugar
¼ teaspoon salt
6 eggs, separated

½ cup lemon juice
1 cup cream, whipped

In a saucepan, combine sugar, salt, egg yolks, and lemon juice. Cook, stirring constantly, until thick. Cool. In a bowl, beat egg whites until peaked. Fold into cooled mixture. Fold in whipped cream. Pour over crumb crust. Sprinkle remaining crumbs on top. Freeze several hours before serving.

NORMA YUTZY, Drakesville, IA

Date Nut Banana Pudding

Cake:

1 cup finely chopped dates
1 teaspoon baking soda
1 cup hot water
1 cup brown sugar

1 tablespoon butter
1 cup flour
1 egg
½ cup nuts

Mix dates, baking soda, and water and let set until cool. Add brown sugar, butter, flour, egg, and nuts. Stir. Pour into greased baking pan. Bake at 350 degrees for 20 to 30 minutes.

Topping:

2 tablespoons butter
1 cup brown sugar
1½ cups water
3 tablespoons Clear Jel or 2 tablespoons cornstarch
2 teaspoons vanilla

1½ teaspoons maple flavoring
2 tablespoons maple syrup
1 (8 ounce) carton frozen whipped topping, thawed
2 to 3 bananas, sliced

In a saucepan, boil butter, brown sugar, water, and Clear Jel for 10 minutes. Add vanilla, maple flavoring, and syrup. When ready to serve, alternate layers of cake, sauce, whipped topping, and bananas.

Mrs. Harvey R. Miller, South Dayton, NY

Classic Pecan Pie

3 eggs, lightly beaten
2 tablespoons butter, melted
1 cup dark corn syrup
1 teaspoon vanilla

1 cup sugar
1 cup pecans
1 unbaked pie shell

In a large bowl, stir eggs, butter, corn syrup, vanilla, and sugar until well blended. Stir in pecans. Pour into pie shell. Bake at 400 degrees for 50 to 55 minutes.

Liz Miller, Decatur, IN

Almond Chip Cookie Bars

1 cup butter
½ cup sugar
½ cup brown sugar
1 teaspoon vanilla or
   almond flavoring

2 cups flour
3 cups baking chips
   (chocolate, butterscotch,
   or peanut butter)
¾ cup sliced almonds

In a bowl, mix together butter, sugar, brown sugar, vanilla, and flour. Spread into 9x13-inch pan. Bake at 350 degrees for 20 to 25 minutes until golden brown. Top with baking chips and return to oven until melted. Spread with spatula. Sprinkle with nuts.

Norma Yutzy, Drakesville, IA

Walnut Wafers

3 eggs
2 cups brown sugar
2 cups black walnuts,
   rolled fine into meal

1 cup flour
Pinch salt
¼ teaspoon baking soda

In a bowl, mix eggs, brown sugar, and walnuts. Add flour, salt, and baking soda. Drop by teaspoonful on cookie sheet. Bake at 350 degrees for 10 minutes or until done.

Judy Zimmerman, East Earl, PA

Mincemeat Cookies

1 cup shortening
1 cup sugar
1 cup brown sugar
3 eggs
3 cups flour
1 teaspoon baking soda

1 teaspoon cinnamon
½ teaspoon ground cloves
½ teaspoon nutmeg
½ teaspoon salt
1 cup mincemeat
1 cup chopped nuts

In a bowl, cream shortening, sugar, and brown sugar. Add eggs and beat until fluffy. In another bowl, sift together flour, baking soda, cinnamon, cloves, nutmeg, and salt. Sift a second time. Add dry mixture to creamed mixture. Mix thoroughly. Add mincemeat and nuts. Drop by teaspoonful on greased baking sheets. Bake at 350 degrees for 10 to 15 minutes.

LENA YODER, McClure, PA

COCOA ALMONDS

6 cups oven-roasted almonds
6 tablespoons butter, melted
1 tablespoon vanilla
½ cup powdered sweetener

⅓ to ½ cup cocoa powder
Extra cocoa powder and
  powdered sweetener

In a large bowl, combine almonds, butter, and vanilla, tossing to coat. In a small bowl, mix sweetener and cocoa powder. Sprinkle over almonds and stir until they are well coated. Pour on a parchment-covered cookie sheet. Bake at 275 degrees for about 1 hour, stirring every 15 minutes. Watch closely during last 15 minutes so that they don't burn. Toss cooled but still warm almonds in additional cocoa powder and powdered sweetener for extra goodness.

NORMA YUTZY, Drakesville, IA

CHOCOLATE MOCHA DUSTED PECANS

2 teaspoons instant
  coffee granules
¾ cup powdered sugar

3 teaspoons cocoa powder
1 cup dark chocolate chips
2 cups toasted pecan halves

Place coffee granules in a plastic zipper bag. Crush with rolling pin until powdery. In a small mixing bowl, mix coffee with powdered sugar and cocoa powder. Set aside. In a saucepan, melt chocolate chips over low heat, stirring until smooth and glossy. Add pecan halves and mix until evenly coated. Add coffee mixture, stirring to toss and coat evenly. Spread on cookie sheet and refrigerate until chocolate is set. Store in airtight container.

"A nice addition to a party table. You can also fill small cellophane bags and add a decorative gift tag to give to your friends."

KATHRYN TROYER, Rutherford, TN

Favorite Snack Mix

6 cups rice or corn
    squares cereal
2½ cups mixed nuts, optional

1 (10 ounce) bag pretzels
¾ cup butter
¾ cup brown sugar

In a large bowl, combine cereal, nuts, and pretzels; set aside. In a saucepan, combine butter and brown sugar; heat until sugar is melted. Coat cereal mixture. Spread on parchment-covered baking sheets and bake at 325 degrees for 8 minutes. Stir, then bake for 8 minutes more.

MARY AND KATIE YODER, Goshen, IN

Thanksgiving Party Mix

1 (10.5 ounce) package
    peanut butter crackers
1 package pretzels
1 cup dry-roasted peanuts
½ cup butter
1 cup sugar
½ cup light corn syrup

1 teaspoon baking soda
2 tablespoons vanilla-
10 ounces chocolate
    coated candies
1 (18.5 ounce) package
    candy corn

In a large bowl, combine crackers, pretzels, and peanuts. In a saucepan, combine butter, sugar, and corn syrup. Bring to a boil over medium heat for 5 minutes. Remove from heat. Add baking soda and vanilla (mixture will foam). Pour over cracker mixture and stir to coat. Pour on greased cookie sheets and bake at 250 degrees for 45 minutes, stirring every 15 minutes. Break apart while warm. Toss with chocolate-coated candies and candy corn. Cool completely and store in airtight container. Makes 16 cups.

MRS. BENJAMIN WICKEY, Monroe, IN

Slush Puppies

1½ cups sugar
1 envelope drink mix
(any flavor)

1½ cups boiling water
8 quarts clean, fluffy snow

Dissolve sugar and drink mix in boiling water. Chill. Form snow into one ball per dish or serving. Pour syrup over top ball and enjoy.

Betty Byler, Smicksburg, PA

Snow Ice Cream

4 to 5 cups clean, fresh snow
1 cup milk

½ cup sugar
½ teaspoon vanilla

Gather clean, fresh snow, but don't pack it down. In a bowl, mix milk, sugar, and vanilla until sugar dissolves. Slowly add the snow, stirring constantly until it is as thick as ice cream.

Judy Zimmerman, East Earl, PA

Maple Syrup Candy

Boil desired amount of maple syrup to 236 degrees on candy thermometer. Remove from heat. Stir while hot until milky in appearance and almost ready to set. Do not stir too long or it will become grainy. Pour into molds. Chill before turning out.

Edna Irene Miller, Arthur, IL

COOKIE EXCHANGE

Each December, a group of friends prepares a cookie exchange. We enjoy a sit-down luncheon of homemade soups, salads, and breads. Each guest brings 8 dozen of one type of Christmas cookie that is different from what others are bringing. You'll end up with 8 dozen different kinds of cookies to take home. The dads will be home babysitting, but they don't seem to mind, considering 8 dozen cookies will be coming home with their wives. We finish the day before leaving with coffee and tea, sampling some of the cookies we received. What fun!

KATHRYN DETWEILER, West Farmington, OH

Homemade Bologna

10 pounds venison burger
  or hamburger
3 cups water
½ cup curing salt
3 tablespoons liquid smoke

4 teaspoons pepper
1 teaspoon onion powder
1¼ cups brown sugar
1½ teaspoons salt
Cheese cubes (optional)

Place meat in large mixing bowl. In another bowl, combine water with curing salt, liquid smoke, pepper, onion powder, brown sugar, and salt. Pour over meat and mix well. Add cheese (if using). Stuff meat into cloth bologna bags. Refrigerate overnight. Bake at 300 degrees for 2½ to 3 hours.

Katie Petersheim, Mifflin, PA

Brine for Venison

7 quarts water
¼ cup baking soda

½ cup vinegar

In a 5-gallon bucket, combine water, baking soda, and vinegar. Add deer meat, being sure it is covered in brine. Let soak at least 12 hours. Remove meat and rinse well with water. This helps to take out the strong, gamey taste.

Clara Yoder, Sugar Grove, PA

HOUSEHOLD TIPS

BEESWAX LIP BALM

¼ cup grated beeswax	2 tablespoons cocoa butter
3 tablespoons coconut oil	1 tablespoon almond oil

Mix ingredients together and heat gently in a double boiler until everything is melted. Pour into small tins or lip balm tubes.

MARYANN KEMPF, Winterset, IA

NATURAL HAIRSPRAY

2 cups boiling water	8 tablespoons rubbing alcohol
8 teaspoons sugar	20 drops essential oil (optional)

In a bowl, blend water and sugar until dissolved. Add rubbing alcohol and essential oil. Pour in a spray bottle. Spritz on hair as needed.

RUTHIE MILLER, Loudonville, OH

WATERING HOUSEPLANTS

Collect rainwater and give it to your houseplants. They will love it!

MARY ELLEN MILLER, Apple Creek, OH

Healthy Tea

I often make a cup of tea in the morning with 3 teaspoons apple cider vinegar with the mother and 1 teaspoon honey in a cup of hot water. I feel this keeps me from getting sick as often with colds and the like.

Iva Yoder, Goshen, IN

Homemade Rehydration Fluid

¼ cup fresh lemon juice
¼ cup maple syrup
½ teaspoon unrefined salt

1 quart water (or replace half of water with coconut water or grape juice)

Thoroughly mix all ingredients together.

To rehydrate infants, give a dropperful every 2 to 3 minutes.

Lydia Miller, Loudonville, OH

Cold and Flu Remedy

1 tablespoon apple cider vinegar
1 tablespoon honey

1 tablespoon lemon juice
½ to 1 cup warm water

Mix together and drink in the morning.

Clara Yoder, Sugar Grove, PA

Homemade Chest Rub

¼ cup coconut oil
8 to 10 drops eucalyptus essential oil

8 to 10 drops lemon essential oil
8 to 10 drops peppermint essential oil

Stir all together, mixing well. Store in glass jar (lemon oil breaks down plastic). Rub a bit on chest and neck at first sign of a cold.

Katurah Miller, Loudonville, OH

YEAR-ROUND

Dairy · Dried Beans
Dried Fruit · Grains · Honey

YEAR-ROUND RECIPES

*"Any housewife, no matter how large her family,
can always get some time alone by doing the dishes."*

MARTHA MILLER, DECATUR, IN

Iced Honey Mocha

Ice
1 cup cold brewed coffee
3 to 5 teaspoons honey
½ tablespoon cocoa powder

3 to 4 tablespoons half
  and half, coconut milk,
  or almond milk

Fill a wide-mouth pint-size mason jar halfway full with ice. Top with coffee, honey, and cocoa powder. Screw lid on mason jar and shake vigorously until cocoa powder is well mixed into the drink. Top with half and half. Mix until blended.

Kathy Nisley, Loudonville, OH

Fruit Punch

2 packages cherry drink mix
2 packages strawberry
  drink mix
4 cups sugar
5½ quarts water

12 ounces frozen orange
  juice concentrate
12 ounces frozen lemonade
  concentrate
1 (2 liter) bottle lemon-
  lime soda pop
Crushed ice

In large container, combine cherry and strawberry drink mixes with sugar. Add water, stirring to dissolve sugar. Add orange juice and lemonade concentrates. Stir until dissolved. When ready to serve, add soda pop and ice.

Mrs. Benjamin Wickey, Monroe, IN

Slushy Punch

2 small boxes
  raspberry gelatin
2 cups sugar
1½ quarts boiling water

46 ounces pineapple juice
1½ quarts cold water
1 (2 liter) bottle lemon-
  lime soda pop

In a bowl, mix gelatin, sugar, and boiling water. Once dissolved, add pineapple juice and cold water. Freeze. Once ready to serve, thaw slightly and add soda pop. Should be slushy when serving.

Mary Ellen Miller, Apple Creek, OH

French Onion Dip

½ cup mayonnaise
½ cup plain yogurt
2 tablespoons grated
  Parmesan cheese

1 teaspoon onion powder
½ teaspoon garlic powder
1 teaspoon parsley
Salt and pepper to taste

In a small bowl, mix all together until smooth. Place into a serving bowl and serve with sliced crunchy veggies or crackers and chips.

JOANNA D. MILLER, Loudonville, OH

Pizza Dip

1 (8 ounce) package cream
  cheese, softened
1 (16 ounce) carton
  sour cream
1½ packages pepperoni,
  chopped

½ onion, chopped
½ teaspoon garlic powder
¼ teaspoon oregano
1 pint pizza sauce
Shredded cheese

Mix together cream cheese, sour cream, pepperoni, onion, garlic powder, and oregano. Pour into 9x13-inch greased glass dish. Top with pizza sauce and cheese. Bake at 350 degrees for 30 minutes until heated through and cheese is melted. Serve with tortilla chips.

MARY BONTRAGER, Middlebury, IN

Smoked Bacon Cheddar 'n' Ranch Cracker Dip

12 ounces cream
cheese, softened
1 cup shredded
cheddar cheese
8 ounces processed cheese
½ cup sour cream
¼ cup butter

¼ cup mayonnaise
½ cup fried and
crumbled bacon
1 tablespoon powdered
ranch seasoning
⅛ teaspoon liquid smoke

In a bowl, blend cream cheese, cheddar, and processed cheese. Add sour cream, butter, and mayonnaise. Stir in bacon crumbles, ranch seasoning, and liquid smoke. It makes a very soft cheese ball–type of dip. You can serve it in a bowl and sprinkle with more bacon or gently shape into a ball and roll in bacon and parsley.

Kathryn Troyer, Rutherford, TN

Fruit Parfait

3 cups oats
½ cup brown sugar
⅛ teaspoon cinnamon
½ cup powdered sugar

1 (8 ounce) package cream
  cheese, softened
1 (32 ounce) container yogurt
1 (16 ounce) container
  whipped topping
Fresh or canned fruit

Mix oats, brown sugar, and cinnamon. Spread on baking sheet and toast at 325 degrees for 15 minutes, stirring once. Place in bottom of serving dish or individual bowls. In a mixing bowl, blend powdered sugar, cream cheese, yogurt, and whipped topping. Spoon over granola. Top with fruit.

MRS. AMANDA BYLER, Curwensville, PA

Baked Oatmeal

6 cups oats
1 tablespoon cinnamon
½ teaspoon salt
1 tablespoon baking powder
1 cup honey

4 eggs
1 cup butter or coconut
  oil, melted
½ cup milk or water
2 teaspoons vanilla

In a bowl, mix all ingredients. Pour in greased 9x13-inch pan. Bake at 350 degrees for 35 to 40 minutes until done.

Fruit variation: You can add 2 cups canned or fresh peaches, blueberries, or raspberries to bottom of pan before adding batter.

Peanut butter variation: Add ½ to 1 cup peanut butter and 1 cup chocolate chips to batter.

MARY ELLEN SCHWARTZ, Mayslick, KY

Easy and Healthy Chocolate Protein Pancakes

2 full scoops chocolate
protein powder
1 cup steel-cut oats
3 teaspoons baking powder
Pinch sea salt

2 eggs
1 cup almond milk
1 teaspoon vanilla extract
Olive oil

Add protein powder, oats, baking powder, and salt to blender. On medium-low speed, blend until oats are pulverized. Add eggs, milk, and vanilla. Blend until smooth. Preheat a nonstick pan over medium heat with a drizzle of olive oil. Pour about ¼ cup batter on pan per pancake. Cook for about 3 minutes, flipping when edges start to look dry. Cook another 2 minutes. Suggest serving 2 pancakes per person topped with sliced strawberries, chocolate chips, and cinnamon. Add maple syrup if desired.

SARAH MILLER, Big Sandy, TN

Ruby's Waffles

3 eggs, separated
1 cup (approx.) meat
broth and/or milk

1 cup flour
3 teaspoons baking powder

In a mixing bowl, mix egg yolks, broth, flour, and baking powder. Beat egg whites until stiff and fold in last. Thin with additional broth if needed. Heat waffle iron, spray with cooking spray, pour batter into the waffle iron, and cook until golden and slightly crispy.

"Great to serve with fresh spring maple syrup."

RUBY BORNTRAGER, Goshen, IN

Grape Nuts Cereal

6 cups whole wheat flour
½ teaspoon salt
½ cup butter
1 cup honey
1 cup maple syrup
1 tablespoon vanilla

½ teaspoon maple flavoring
2 cups sour milk (or add
  1 tablespoon vinegar
  to sweet milk)
½ tablespoon baking soda

In a mixing bowl, combine flour and salt; set aside. In a saucepan, melt butter. Add honey and maple syrup, stirring. Add vanilla, maple flavoring, milk, and baking soda. Add flour mixture, stirring well. Pour into a cake pan. Bake at 350 degrees for 20 to 25 minutes until browned and center springs back. Cool. Crumble finely. Spread on baking sheet. Dry in a 250- to 275-degree oven for around 30 minutes, stirring often until dry.

ELIZABETH Y. MILLER, Middlefield, OH

Granola

8 cups gluten-free quick oats
4 cups crispy rice cereal
1 cup brown rice flour
1 cup brown sugar
1 teaspoon sea salt

1 teaspoon baking soda
2 cups coconut oil, melted
2 teaspoons vanilla or
  maple flavoring

In a large bowl, combine oats, cereal, flour, brown sugar, salt, and baking soda. Add melted oil and vanilla and mix well. Bake on cookie sheets at 300 degrees for 20 to 30 minutes until golden brown and crispy.

For variation, you can sprinkle liberally with chocolate chips after removing from oven. You can also add ½ cup baking molasses and/or 1 cup coconut before baking.

JULIA TROYER, Fredericksburg, OH

Six-Week Bran Muffins

2 cups boiling water
4 cups bran cereal
1 cup butter
2½ cups brown sugar
4 eggs
1 quart buttermilk

5 cups flour
3 tablespoons baking soda
1 tablespoon salt
2 cups 100% bran
2 cups raisins

Pour boiling water over bran cereal and let stand. In an extra-large mixing bowl, cream butter and brown sugar. Add eggs, cereal mixture, and buttermilk. In a bowl, sift flour, baking soda, and salt. Add 100% bran. Fold dry ingredients into wet mixture until moistened throughout. Mix in raisins. Put batter in refrigerator in a tightly covered container. Do not bake for at least a day. The batter can be kept up to 6 weeks in the refrigerator. To bake, place batter in lined muffin tins, and bake at 375 degrees for 15 minutes.

"So handy to have batter ready for fresh breakfast muffins."

Mrs. Lloyd Kuefer, Kincardine, Ontario

Health Bread

2 cups bran flakes or all-bran cereal	1 cup raisins
2 cups buttermilk	2 teaspoons baking soda
4 teaspoons molasses	2 cups flour
	¼ cup sweetener of choice

Combine all ingredients in a large bowl. Pour into a large, greased loaf pan or 2 small loaf pans. Bake at 350 degrees for 45 to 60 minutes.

David C. P. Schwartz, Galesburg, KS

Soft White Bread

3 tablespoons yeast	1 tablespoon salt
3¾ cups warm water	2 eggs
6 tablespoons sugar or brown sugar	10 cups (approx.) flour, divided
6 tablespoons margarine	

In a large bowl, mix yeast, warm water, and sugar until well dissolved. Let sit about 5 minutes. Add margarine, salt, eggs, and 5 cups flour. Mix well. Slowly work in remaining 5 cups flour until soft and tacky but not sticky. Let rise 10 minutes. Knead. Let rise 10 more minutes. Knead. Let rise a third time for 20 minutes. Divide into 2 greased loaf pans. Let rise. Bake at 350 degrees for 20 to 30 minutes.

Barbara A. Schwartz, Geneva, IN

Multigrain Bread

6 cups warm water
3 eggs
¾ cup sorghum molasses
1 cup olive oil
1 tablespoon apple
   cider vinegar
2 tablespoons lecithin
½ cup instant potato flakes
4 cups freshly ground
   whole wheat flour

1 cup quick oats
¾ cup rye flour
¾ cup spelt flour
¾ cup cornmeal
4 tablespoons instant yeast
4 tablespoons gluten
4 tablespoons flaxseed meal
6 teaspoons salt
8 cups whole wheat
   flour, divided

Put warm water, eggs, molasses, oil, vinegar, lecithin, and potato flakes in mixing bowl (I use a Bosch mixer). Mix with whisk beater. Meanwhile, in a large bowl, mix 4 cups whole wheat flour, oats, rye flour, spelt flour, cornmeal, yeast, gluten, flaxseed meal, and salt. Add to liquid mixture and whisk for 5 to 10 minutes. Change beater to dough hook. Add 1 cup whole wheat flour every 2 to 3 minutes of mixing until dough leaves side of bowl, adding approximately 8 cups flour. Dump dough out on a floured surface. Cut into 6 equal pieces. Knead each one a few times. Put each into a greased bread pan. Let rise until double. Bake at 350 degrees for 45 minutes. Makes 6 loaves.

Anna M. Byler, Commodore, PA

Good and Easy Pizza Dough

1 package (1 tablespoon) yeast
1 cup warm water
1 teaspoon sugar

2½ cups flour
2 tablespoons oil
Toppings of your choice

Dissolve yeast in water. Stir in sugar, flour, and oil. Beat 20 strokes. Spread dough in pizza pan and let rest for 5 to 10 minutes. Top with favorite pizza toppings and bake at 450 degrees for 15 to 20 minutes.

Rachel Kuefer, Kincardine, Ontario

Pepperoni Bread

1 pound (or 1 recipe) pizza dough	½ teaspoon parsley
5 tablespoons butter, melted	¼ teaspoon seasoned salt
¼ teaspoon garlic powder	1 to 2 cups pepperoni
	2 cups mozzarella cheese

Roll dough out to 10x15-inch rectangle. In a small bowl, mix together butter, garlic powder, parsley, and seasoned salt. Spread about 3 tablespoons butter over dough. Layer pepperoni on dough. Top with cheese. Start from short end and roll up dough like a jelly roll. Fold ends under and seal. Place seam-side down on greased baking sheet. Brush top with remaining butter. Bake at 350 degrees for 30 minutes. Slice and enjoy while warm.

Norma Yutzy, Drakesville, IA

Pizza Loaves

1½ pounds ground meat	1 cup chopped onion
½ teaspoon garlic powder	1 can sliced jalapeños, drained
½ teaspoon salt	1 can pizza sauce
1 loaf bread, halved lengthwise	4 cups shredded cheese
1 (8 ounce) jar cheese sauce	½ cup Parmesan cheese
1 can mushrooms, drained	

In a skillet, brown meat and drain. Stir in garlic powder and salt. Place bread on foil. Spread with cheese sauce. Top with meat, mushrooms, onion, and jalapeños. Drizzle with pizza sauce. Top with cheeses. Wrap up in foil and bake at 350 degrees for 18 minutes. Loaded loaves can also be refrigerated or frozen before baking.

Norma Yutzy, Drakesville, IA

Broccoli and Cauliflower Casserole

16 ounces broccoli and
   cauliflower frozen mix
1 can cream of
   mushroom soup

1 cup uncooked instant rice
1 small jar cheese sauce

Mix all together in a casserole. Bake at 350 degrees for 30 minutes or until bubbly.

CRYSTAL ROPP, Kalona, IA

Best-Ever Corn Casserole

2 cups whole kernel corn
2 cups cream-style corn
1 small onion, chopped
1 (8 ounce) container
   sour cream

1 package corn muffin mix
Salt and pepper to taste
Dried parsley

In a bowl, combine all ingredients and pour in a greased casserole. Bake at 350 degrees for 45 minutes. Yields 10 servings.

MARY ELLEN SCHWARTZ, Mayslick, KY

Winter Stew

1 package stew meat
1 to 2 tablespoons flour
1 tablespoon oil
2 cups chopped potatoes
1 cup chopped carrots
1 cup chopped turnips

1 cup chopped celery
1 cup chopped onions
½ teaspoon thyme
½ teaspoon sage
½ teaspoon poultry
   seasoning

Toss meat in a bit of flour to coat. Place meat in large kettle or dutch oven with oil and brown. Cover with water. Simmer for 1½ hours. Add potatoes, carrots, turnips, celery, onions, thyme, sage, and poultry seasoning. Cook 30 minutes more, or until meat and vegetables are tender. Thicken if desired with flour and milk. Serve alone or with biscuits, dumplings, or slices of bread.

WANDA E. BRUNSTETTER

Lentil Soup

1 cup lentils
2½ cups water
2 beef bouillon cubes
1 teaspoon oregano
1 tablespoon curry powder

½ onion, chopped
2¾ cups tomato juice
½ pound diced ham or
   browned hamburger
1 bay leaf

Combine all ingredients in a large saucepan and bring to a boil. Simmer until lentils are soft. Remove bay leaf before serving.

ANNA M. BYLER, Commodore, PA

Split Pea Soup

½ pound green or
   yellow split peas
4 cups water
1 ham hock or meaty
   ham bone

⅓ cup diced carrots
⅓ cup diced celery
⅓ cup diced onion
½ teaspoon salt

Sort, wash, and drain split peas. Combine all ingredients in kettle with tight-fitting lid. Bring to a boil. Reduce heat and simmer, covered, for 2 hours, stirring occasionally. Remove ham hock or bone. Cool slightly. Cut meat off bone and dice. Add to soup and heat thoroughly. Note: Split peas do not require soaking.

SARAH TROYER, Mercer, PA

Old-Fashioned Cream of Tomato Soup

1 tablespoon chicken base
1 cup water
1 ounce butter
2 tablespoons sugar
1 tablespoon chopped onion
1 (16 ounce) can diced
  tomatoes in puree

1 (16 ounce) can
  crushed tomatoes
½ teaspoon baking soda
1 (8 ounce) container heavy
  whipping cream
8 ounces liquid coffee
  creamer or half and half,
  or 4 ounces heavy cream
  with 4 ounces water

In saucepan, combine chicken base, water, butter, sugar, and onion. Simmer until onions are clear. Add tomatoes and baking soda. Stir well. Add heavy whipping cream and creamer. Heat and serve.

JOANN MILLER, Fredericktown, OH

Taco Soup

1 pound hamburger
1 cup chili beans, undrained
2 small onions, chopped
3 cups tomato juice
¼ cup brown sugar

1 package taco seasoning
Shredded cheese
Sour cream
Tortilla chips

In a saucepan, brown hamburger. Add beans, onions, juice, brown sugar, and seasoning. Simmer for about 1 hour until thickened. Serve with shredded cheese, sour cream, and chips.

MARY ANN YUTZY, Bloomfield, IA

TACO PIE

BASE:

2 pounds hamburger,
   browned
1 pint canned pinto beans
1 pint pizza sauce
1 package taco seasoning

2 cups flour
1 tablespoon baking powder
⅓ cup vegetable oil
1½ cups milk

In a bowl, mix hamburger, beans, pizza sauce, and seasoning. Spread into large casserole or cake pan. In another bowl, blend together flour, baking powder, oil, and milk. Pour over hamburger mixture. Bake at 375 degrees for 30 to 40 minutes, until an inserted knife comes out clean. Cool slightly for 10 minutes. Just before serving, add toppings.

TOPPINGS:

1 small head lettuce,
   chopped
1 to 2 tomatoes, chopped

Cheese
Ranch dressing

Lay lettuce over baked pie. Add generous amount of tomatoes and cheese. Drizzle ranch dressing over top. Serve.

CRYSTAL ROPP, Kalona, IA

BBQ Meatballs

1¼ pounds hamburger

2 cups ketchup

½ teaspoon garlic powder

1¼ cups brown sugar

2 teaspoons onion powder

¾ teaspoon liquid smoke

Form hamburger into 30 (1-inch) meatballs. In a skillet with a little water, steam meatballs about 15 minutes. Put into baking dish. In bowl, blend ketchup, garlic powder, brown sugar, onion powder, and liquid smoke. Pour sauce over meatballs. Bake at 350 degrees for 20 minutes or until sauce is bubbly.

Mary Bontrager, Middlebury, IN

Ham Loaf

1½ pounds ground ham
1½ pounds ground
  pork sausage

5 eggs
1½ cups fine cracker crumbs
1½ cups ketchup

In a large bowl, mix ham, sausage, eggs, crumbs, and ketchup. Mold into little loaves of ⅓ to ½ cup each. Make a cross or X on top of each loaf. Bake at 350 degrees for 30 minutes. Remove from oven. Spread with sauce. Return to oven for 10 minutes. (You can also bake the mixture in 1 to 2 large loaves. Adjust time to at least 45 minutes for first bake.)

SAUCE:

½ cup brown sugar
1 tablespoon mustard

1 tablespoon vinegar

Mix all until smooth.

ELLA ARLENE YODER, Arcola, IL

Hot Dog Surprise

1 teaspoon chopped onion
2 cups chopped hot dogs
2 cups chopped ham
½ cup grated cheese
2 hard-boiled eggs, chopped
2 tablespoons pickle relish

3 tablespoons ketchup
1 teaspoon mustard
3 tablespoons mayonnaise
  (optional)
Hot dog rolls

In a large bowl, mix all ingredients except rolls. Put mixture in rolls. Wrap in foil and bake at 350 degrees for 12 minutes.

FEENIE BEILER, Delta, PA

Snow Caps

1 pound hot dogs
2 tablespoons finely
chopped onions

10 cups prepared
mashed potatoes
Shredded American cheese

Split hot dogs lengthwise and place in baking pan. Combine onions with mashed potatoes and pile on top of hot dogs. Top with cheese. Bake at 350 degrees for 20 to 25 minutes.

ELLA MILLER, Big Prairie, OH

5-Star Casserole

2 pounds hamburger
1 medium onion, chopped
2 (10.5 ounce) cans or 1 pint
cream of chicken soup
2 (10.5 ounce) cans or 1
pint cheese soup

2 (10.5 ounce) cans or 1
pint tomato soup
2 (10.5 ounce) cans or 1
pint mushroom soup
2 cups water
1 bag shell noodles

In a skillet, cook hamburger and onion until done. In a large bowl, mix chicken soup, cheese soup, tomato soup, and mushroom soup. Add water. Mix in hamburger. In a saucepan, cook noodles according to package directions. Drain. Mix noodles into soup mixture. Pour into large baking dish. Bake at 350 degrees for 1 hour. Serve hot. Option: Mix in some tender cooked carrots, peas, or beans before baking.

"Children love this one."
MRS. LLOYD KUEFER, Kincardine, Ontario

Yumasetta Casserole

2 pounds hamburger
1 medium onion, chopped
1 package medium noodles
1 pint canned or frozen peas
1 can cream of
   mushroom soup

1 can cream of chicken soup
1 can condensed tomato soup
Salt and pepper to taste
1 pound processed cheese

Brown hamburger and onion in a skillet. In a saucepan, cook noodles in hot water until just starting to get tender. Combine hamburger, onion, noodles, peas, mushroom soup, chicken soup, and tomato soup and season with salt and pepper. Put into 9x13-inch casserole. Top with slices of processed cheese. Bake at 250 to 300 degrees for 1 hour.

MARY JOYCE PETERSHEIM, Fredericktown, OH

Marshmallow Crunchies

2 tablespoons margarine
38 to 40 regular large
   marshmallows

6 cups crisp rice cereal

Spray 9x13-inch pan with nonstick cooking spray or brush with melted butter. In a large saucepan, melt margarine over low heat. Add marshmallows, stirring constantly until completely melted. Remove from heat and stir in cereal until evenly coated. Spread into prepared pan using a buttered spatula. Cool and cut into squares.

Crystal Ropp, Kalona, IA

Our Favorite Bars

1 cup butter
1 cup coconut or vegetable oil
1 cup peanut butter
2½ cups raw sugar
¾ cup sorghum
6 eggs
2 teaspoons vanilla

2 teaspoons baking soda
2 teaspoons baking powder
2 cups whole wheat flour
2 cups white flour
4 cups oats
2 cups chocolate chips

In a bowl, beat together butter, oil, peanut butter, sugar, sorghum, eggs, and vanilla. Add baking soda, baking powder, whole wheat flour, white flour, and oats. Mix well. Add chocolate chips, mixing well. Divide into two 9x13-inch pans. Bake at 350 degrees for 20 minutes until set. Don't overbake.

"These bars are soft and loaded with flavor."

Norma Yutzy, Drakesville, IA

Caramel Cake

Cake:

1 cup egg whites
¼ teaspoon salt
1 teaspoon cream of tartar
2 teaspoons maple flavoring
1¼ cups sugar, divided
¾ cup flour

In a bowl, beat egg whites, salt, cream of tartar, and maple flavoring to soft peaks. Add ¾ cup sugar 1 tablespoon at a time and beat until stiff. In a small bowl, sift together flour and remaining ½ cup sugar. Fold into egg whites. Bake at 350 degrees in a 9x13-inch baking pan for 20 minutes. Cool.

Frosting:

1 (8 ounce) package cream
    cheese, softened
⅔ cup brown sugar
1 teaspoon vanilla
½ teaspoon salt
1 (8 ounce) container
    whipped topping

In a bowl, cream together cream cheese, brown sugar, vanilla, and salt. Fold in whipped topping. Spread over cooled cake.

Caramel Topping:

1 cup brown sugar
½ cup butter
1 cup sour cream

In a saucepan, boil together brown sugar and butter. Cool slightly. Add sour cream. Spread over frosting.

Option: You can blend frosting and caramel into one spread.

Norma Yutzy, Drakesville, IA

CHEESECAKE PIE

1 (8 ounce) package cream
  cheese, softened
1 (8 ounce) carton sour cream
¾ cup milk

1 small package instant
  pudding of choice
1 (9 inch) graham
  cracker pie shell

In a mixing bowl, cream together cream cheese and sour cream. Mix in milk and pudding. Pour into pie shell. Top with your choice of favorite pie filling, fresh fruit, or other toppings.

RACHEL KUEFER, Kincardine, Ontario

DERBY PIE

4 eggs, beaten
1 cup light corn syrup
1 cup brown sugar
1 teaspoon vanilla

½ cup butter, melted
½ cup chopped pecans
½ cup chocolate chips
1 (9 inch) unbaked pie shell

In a bowl, mix eggs, corn syrup, brown sugar, vanilla, and butter. Put pecans and chocolate chips into pie shell. Pour syrup over top. Bake at 325 degrees for 30 to 45 minutes until the middle has just a light wobbly shake. Very good served with vanilla ice cream while still warm.

"I have a bakery, and we make these Derby Pies the week in May of the Kentucky Derby horse race in Louisville. Very popular!"

LORENE BYLER, Irvington, KY

CHERRIES IN THE SNOW

CRUST:

1 cup flour
¼ cup sugar

¼ cup melted butter
½ cup nuts (optional)

In a bowl, combine flour, sugar, and butter. Mix in nuts. Spread in an 8-inch square pan or a 9-inch pie pan. Bake at 350 degrees for 15 minutes. Cool.

FILLING:

2 cups powdered sugar
1 (8 ounce) package cream
    cheese, softened

1 teaspoon vanilla
2 cups cream, whipped
1 quart cherry pie filling

In a bowl, combine powdered sugar, cream cheese, and vanilla. Fold into whipped cream. Spread cream cheese filling over crust. Top with pie filling.

RUTH M. YODER, Berlin, PA

FRY PIES

9 cups flour
1 teaspoon salt
3 cups shortening

2 cups water
Pie filling of choice

In a large bowl, combine flour and salt. Cut in shortening until crumbly. Add water a little at a time until flour is moistened and you can form into small balls. Roll out a ball as thin as possible. Cut 4-inch circle using a dish or other template. Place a spoonful of filling near the middle. Fold dough in half and seal edges. Deep-fry in oil at 300 degrees until lightly browned. When cooled, coat with glaze.

GLAZE:

2 pounds powdered sugar
1 cup warm water

Vanilla

In a bowl, gently mix powdered sugar, warm water, and vanilla until smooth.

RACHEL KUEFER, Kincardine, Ontario

CHERRY TORTE

1 yellow or white cake mix	1 quart cherry pie filling
1 stick butter, melted	¾ cup nuts

In a bowl, combine cake mix and butter. Press two-thirds of mixture into bottom of greased 9x13-inch pan. Cover with pie filling. Sprinkle with remaining crumbs and top with nuts. Bake at 350 degrees for 45 minutes. Serve with whipped cream or ice cream.

ELLA MILLER, Big Prairie, OH

S'MORES CHEESECAKE BARS

2 packages graham crackers, crushed	2 eggs
1 cup sugar, divided	1 can condensed milk
¾ cup melted butter	1 cup mini marshmallows
2 (8 ounce) packages cream cheese, softened	1 cup chocolate chips

Mix graham crackers, ½ cup sugar, and butter; press firmly into a large cookie sheet. In a bowl, mix cream cheese, remaining ½ cup sugar, eggs, and condensed milk until smooth and spread on top of crumbs. Bake at 350 degrees for 18 minutes until light brown and set, then put marshmallows on top and bake another 3 to 4 minutes. Melt chocolate chips and drizzle over the top.

MARILYN LAMBRIGHT, Goshen, IN

Chocolate Kisses Macaroon Cookies

⅓ cup butter, softened
3 ounces cream
   cheese, softened
¾ cup sugar
1 egg yolk
2 teaspoons almond flavoring
2 teaspoons orange juice

1¼ cups flour
2 teaspoons baking powder
¼ teaspoon salt
5 cups sweetened
   coconut, divided
Chocolate Kisses candy

In a bowl, beat butter, cream cheese, and sugar until well blended. Add egg yolk, almond flavoring, and orange juice, and beat well. Add flour, baking powder, and salt. Stir in 3 cups of coconut last. Cover, then refrigerate until firm enough to handle. Shape into balls and roll in remaining 2 cups of coconut. Bake at 350 degrees until lightly browned. Immediately press 1 chocolate kiss onto each cookie. Carefully remove from cookie sheet and cool right away. Makes 48 cookies.

KATHRYN DETWEILER, West Farmington, OH

Delicious Lemon Cookies

1 (8 ounce) package cream
   cheese, softened
4 eggs, beaten
¼ cup water
2 packages lemon cake mix

½ cup plus 2
   tablespoons flour
⅔ cup oil
Powdered sugar

In a bowl, beat together cream cheese and eggs. Mix in water. Add cake mix, flour, and oil. Mix well. Put a spoonful in powdered sugar, tossing until coated. Press gently with fingers to flatten when on pan. Bake at 350 degrees for 10 to 12 minutes. Makes 3½ to 4 dozen cookies.

These lemon cookies stay fresh in a plastic container with wax paper between the layers. They also freeze well for several months.

KATIE YODER, Goshen, IN

Ice Cream

1 cup sugar
½ cup instant Clear Jel
5 eggs, beaten
2 teaspoons vanilla

Pinch salt
¾ cup heavy cream
1 quart milk
1 can evaporated milk

In a large bowl, mix sugar and Clear Jel. Add eggs, vanilla, salt, cream, milk, and evaporated milk. Pour into ice cream maker canister and freeze.

Note: This recipe uses raw eggs.

Feenie Beiler, Delta, PA

Butter Pecan Frozen Custard

Candied Pecans:

1 cup pecan halves
1 tablespoon butter

1 tablespoon sweetener of choice

Toast pecans in a nonstick pan with butter and sweetener over medium heat until just golden brown. Watch carefully. Cool.

Ice Cream:

2 cups half and half
2 cups milk
2 eggs
2 egg yolks
⅓ cup xylitol or ⅔ cup raw sugar
2 tablespoons salted butter
2 tablespoons natural peanut butter

1 tablespoon vegetable glycerin
¼ teaspoon salt
¼ teaspoon maple flavoring
⅛ teaspoon stevia (or adjust to taste)
1 cup heavy whipping cream
2 teaspoons vanilla

In a blender, blend half and half, milk, eggs, yolks, xylitol, butter, peanut butter, glycerin, salt, maple flavoring, and stevia. Pour into heavy saucepan and cook mixture over medium heat until it starts to bubble, whisking often. Remove from heat and add heavy cream and vanilla, blending again until smooth. Chill the mixture completely. Freeze using ice cream freezer. When finished, pour into sealable container and fold in pecans. Serves 8.

RANAE YODER, Kalona, IA

Traditional Pineapple Rings

1 can sweetened condensed milk
1 can pineapple slices

½ cup whipped topping
1 small jar maraschino cherries

In a saucepan, place unopened can sweetened condensed milk, completely covered in water, and cook for 4½ hours. Make sure the can does not have a pull tab. You'll need to open both ends when evaporated milk has finished cooking. Push pudding out of can and cut ⅛-inch-thick slices. Place slices of pudding on top of pineapple slices. Add dab of whipped topping on top of pudding slice. Put a cherry on top of whipped topping.

"Attractive and yummy!"

MARY AND KATIE YODER, Goshen, IN

Granola Bars

2 cups quick oats
2 cups old-fashioned oats
1 cup unsweetened coconut
½ cup dried cranberries
    or raisins
½ cup slivered almonds
1 cup dark chocolate or
    sugar-free chips

¼ cup honey
¼ cup butter
¼ cup olive oil
¼ cup maple syrup
¾ cup peanut butter
2 teaspoons vanilla

In a large bowl, combine quick oats, old-fashioned oats, coconut, cranberries, almonds, and chocolate chips. In a saucepan, bring honey, butter, olive oil, maple syrup, and peanut butter to a boil. Add vanilla. Pour over dry ingredients. Mix well and press into a 9x13-inch pan. Cool before cutting. Store in a cool, dry place.

Iva Yoder, Goshen, IN

Healthy Energy Bites

1 cup oats
⅓ cup unsweetened coconut
½ cup ground flaxseed
3 tablespoons chia seeds

½ cup chocolate chips
    (72% cacao)
½ cup unsweetened
    peanut butter
⅓ cup honey
1 teaspoon vanilla

Mix all ingredients in a bowl. Form into balls. Store in refrigerator.

Mary Ellen Wengerd, Campbellsville, KY

MUSTARD PRETZELS

1½ cups butter, melted
1 squirt mustard
2 tablespoons
  Worcestershire sauce
2 pounds pretzels

¼ cup powdered sugar
1 teaspoon ground mustard
1 teaspoon garlic powder
1 teaspoon turmeric

In a bowl, mix butter, mustard, and Worcestershire sauce. Pour over pretzels and spread on a baking sheet. Bake at 300 degrees for 30 minutes. In small bowl, mix powdered sugar, ground mustard, garlic powder, and turmeric. Sprinkle over pretzels and toss to coat.

"We all like these in our lunch buckets."

ANNA HERSHBERGER, Fredericksburg, OH

Banana Boats

Bananas (still firm)   Chocolate chips
Peanut butter   Large marshmallows

Plan 1 banana per person. Peel banana. Slice a bit off bottom curve of banana so it sits flat with ends up. Carve a groove into top of banana. Fill groove with peanut butter. Sprinkle with chocolate chips and press in a bit. Poke 1 or 2 marshmallows on a toothpick and then poke into banana as the boat mast.

Crystal Ropp, Kalona, IA

Turkey Drumsticks

2 tablespoons butter   Caramel squares
¾ cup chocolate chips   Pretzel rods

In a saucepan, stir together butter and chocolate chips until melted. Shape caramel on one end of pretzel rod. Dip in chocolate to coat half of the rod. Repeat with each caramel and rod.

Feenie Beiler, Delta, PA

White Party Mix

3 cups rice squares cereal
3 cups corn squares cereal
3 cups oat rounds cereal
2 cups dry-roasted peanuts
2 cups pretzels

1 pound white chocolate coating
1 pound chocolate-coated candies

In a large bowl, combine cereals, peanuts, and pretzels. Melt white chocolate in double boiler or microwave. Pour over mixture and stir to coat well. Add candies and mix in before chocolate cools. Spread onto cookie sheets to dry and harden. Break into pieces. Delicious and festive!

RACHEL KUEFER, Kincardine, Ontario

Peanut Butter Popcorn

12 cups popcorn, lightly salted and still warm
¼ cup butter, melted

3 tablespoons peanut butter
3 tablespoons brown sugar

Pour freshly popped popcorn into a large bowl. In a bowl or saucepan, blend butter, peanut butter, and brown sugar until liquefied. Pour over popcorn. Toss lightly. Serve immediately.

CRYSTAL ROPP, Kalona, IA

Kettle Corn

¹/₃ cup canola oil

½ cup large popcorn kernels

Pinch popcorn salt

¹/₃ cup sugar

Put oil and popcorn in popper on stovetop. Add salt. Over medium heat, keep stirring popcorn. When it starts to pop, add sugar. Continue stirring until it's done popping.

Note: Large popcorn doesn't burn and stick to the bottom.

"Fun for picnics and camping."

Mary and Katie Yoder, Goshen, IN

Yogurt

2 tablespoons plain gelatin
1 cup cold water
1 gallon milk

2 cups sugar
1 cup yogurt with
active cultures

Soak gelatin in cold water. Heat milk to 190 degrees. Cool to 130 degrees. Add sugar, yogurt, and soaked gelatin. Beat with eggbeater. Cover and set in a warm place for 4 to 6 hours or until set up. Save 1 cup for next batch. Portion into small containers and chill overnight until fully set.

To flavor: Add 1 can pie filling or 2 boxes flavored gelatin soaked in 2 cups hot water to batch of yogurt.

Barbara A. Schwartz, Geneva, IN

Hominy

8 pounds large popcorn kernels
½ pound baking soda

In a large canner or stockpot, soak popcorn and baking soda covered in warm water for 24 hours. Cook for 5 to 7 hours on low, stirring every 20 minutes or so. Add water often enough to keep corn covered. When corn is soft enough, rinse well in strainer and put back in canner for 2 to 3 days. Rinse with water twice a day.

To can, pack into pint jars, cover with hot water, and cold-pack for 1½ hours.

EMMA A. HERSHBERGER, Apple Creek, OH

Amish Peanut Butter Spread

2 cups brown sugar
1 cup water
1 teaspoon maple extract

2 cups peanut butter
1 (16 ounce) jar
    marshmallow crème

In saucepan, combine brown sugar, water, and maple extract and bring to a boil. Blend peanut butter and marshmallow crème. Then blend both mixtures together until smooth. Serve as a spread on bread or crackers.

SALOMA STUTZMAN, Navarre, OH

Play Dough

2½ cups flour
½ cup salt
1 tablespoon cooking oil

1 tablespoon alum
2 cups boiling water
Food coloring (optional)

In a bowl, mix flour, salt, oil, and alum. Add water. Mix well. When cooled, knead like bread dough. Will keep for months if stored in an airtight container.

Mrs. Rebecca Byler, Spartansburg, PA

Yak Play Dough

1½ cups water
2 (8 ounce) bottles
  white school glue

2 teaspoons Borax
1 cup warm water
15 to 20 drops food coloring

Mix 1½ cups water with glue. In a separate bowl, dissolve Borax in warm water. Add food coloring. Mix into glue mixture very quickly with your hands until smooth.

"This is a great pastime for little ones and adults to enjoy together. Just make sure children don't have on good clothes because it is a challenge to get out if the dough gets on the clothes."

Hannah Schrock, Salem, MO

INDEX OF CONTRIBUTORS

Index of Recipes by Key Ingredients

Almonds

Apples — includes apple cider, apple juice, apple pie filling, and applesauce

Asparagus

Bacon

Pasta/Noodles

Peaches

Peanut Butter

Peanuts

Peas

Oranges – includes orange juice

Parmesan Cheese

Pecans